HOW TO AVOID

BAG LADY
SYNDROME
[B.L.S.]

A Strong Woman's Guide
to Financial Peace of Mind

Lance Drucker, ChFC®, CLU®
President & CEO, Drucker Wealth Management

ISBN: Hardcover / 978-1-939758-99-6
ISBN: Paperback / 978-0-692-29657-8
ISBN: eBook / 978-0-692-29658-5

For information contact:
Lance Drucker
Drucker Wealth Management
212-681-0460

Library of Congress Control Number: 2014916815

Cover design by Andrew Brice

To the women (and one guy)
in my life who have shaped me;

My mom Elaine for teaching me about warmth and compassion;

My sister Dawn for teaching me about love of family;

My mother-in-law Toby who has taught me about inner strength and commitment to a spouse;

My daughter Gabby for teaching me about laughter and strength;

My son Gideon for teaching me about passion and commitment to the things we believe in;

And most importantly to my wife Beth who has taught me about love and without whom, nothing else would matter.

Finally, to my two Labrador Retriever girls who make me want to be the man they think I am.

CONTENTS

CONTENTS

CHAPTER 1

Does Your Money Keep You Tossing and Turning at Night?

Money, if it does not bring you happiness, will at least help you be miserable in comfort.

—HELEN GURLEY BROWN

What do you enjoy? What are you good at? What can you make money doing? The intersection of these three points defines your perfect job. I'm pretty lucky, as I found my perfect calling as the owner of the wealth management firm that my dad founded in 1959—Drucker Wealth Management (DWM). What's unique about our firm is that over 70 percent of our clientele are women. I'm often asked what led us to develop such an expertise in helping our female clients achieve their financial peace of mind. The answer to that question starts with a story.

Just over a decade ago, my wife and I were enjoying a ski vacation with our children in Vermont. We had been hitting the slopes for several days without interruption from the real world. The skies were blue, as only February Vermont skies can be, and the powder was light and fresh that year. It seemed to be one of those trips destined to make the "Best of Family Vacations" list. And then one afternoon we returned to our hotel room and discovered fifteen missed messages on my phone. My father-in-law had had a stroke.

Seymour, my wife's father, had been a successful business executive for thirty years before he and my mother-in-law decided to try a new adventure—purchasing a bagel store in New Jersey with another couple. The two couples ran the store together happily and successfully for five years, facing the unique kinds of challenges and enjoying the special brand of camaraderie often only small business owners come to know.

A few years into my parents-in-law's venture, I had suggested selling the store while it and everyone who ran it were in good physical and financial shape. "But we love our customers," they all said. "We're having too much fun, and there's still more to be had!" You really can't argue with your in-laws and their business partners. Nor could I argue that they weren't still all fit and feisty. And then, completely out of the blue, that stroke hit Seymour.

Weeks after lying in coma and finally coming to, my father-in-law spent some time in a nursing home and then in a physical rehabilitation facility. Eventually, after regaining a satisfactory level of health and mobility, he was released to the care of my wife's mother, Toby. Of course, we were all beyond relieved and thrilled at Seymour's recovery, but he would not be able to go back to work—ever.

Of course, Toby, with her boundless energy, helped her husband at home and then attended to business at the bagel shop. She and her friends stayed committed and were able to keep things running for a while, but Seymour's hard work and business acumen were missed—and business eventually began to suffer. Within a year of Seymour's stroke and subsequent hospitalization, the bagel shop had to be sold in a fire sale, for much less than everyone had planned on.

Toby is still caring for Seymour in their home. In addition to attending to her husband's healthcare needs, she is in charge of paying the bills, balancing the checkbook, and evaluating their continually changing insurance needs. As her son-in-law, I have helped her through each new challenge. I handle her financial planning needs, and my wife, of course, provides her with unwavering emotional support. Despite the sudden and drastic life change, Toby is, of course, more than grateful to have Seymour around to complain about. She counts each day they have together as a blessing, and they continue to share many more joys than they do headaches.

But the truth is, things could have worked out better for Toby. As a result of choices they made during their life together, Toby and Seymour's financial situation was as precarious as Sy's health. The truth is, for many women, learning to tackle a whole slew of new financial responsibilities can often come at a time when they are also dealing with the greatest health challenges of their lives (either their own or their spouse's), or with grief.

According to a study conducted by the National Center for Women and Retirement Research in 2007, 90 percent of married women will be solely responsible for handling finances at some point in their lives, either because of divorce or because of the simple fact that they outlive men. In my thirty years of experience, I have found that 100 percent of single women need to be both the hunter as well as the gatherer.

We have found that the optimal time to start addressing your financial needs is now. If you have the time, knowledge, interest, and financial acumen, then there is nothing wrong with going it alone. Fortunately for Drucker Wealth Management, many women have decided that they would prefer to have a qualified, professional guide through the jungle of financial planning. Good advice can help make life a little easier when the unexpected occurs. It can protect you from falling into common financial traps, and it can undoubtedly improve your chances of maintaining financial security over the long term.

My own mother certainly wasn't expecting the life changes she had to face—and she had been married her entire life to a financial planner, to my father and founder of Drucker Wealth Management, Bernie Drucker. My dad recently passed after having suffered from Alzheimer's disease for the past five years. Soon after my father's diagnosis, my mother, Elaine (much like my wife's mother, Toby) was forced to take over all the household financial responsibilities, as well as make major medical decisions.

My mom had always paid the bills and, in fact, ran a budgeting service for many of my dad's clients, but she still wasn't totally prepared for all of the financial decisions that cropped up after my father's passing. Fortunately for her, my father had done a wonderful job of accumulating assets. He was a master at what he did, which is one of the reasons I wanted to work with him every day. My mother is alone now, but she is financially independent, and she makes the most of her time and money. As a result of the decades of financial planning that my father put in place, my mom has financial peace of mind that unfortunately my mother-in-law does not.

One of my favorite movies is *My Big Fat Greek Wedding* because it illustrates the warmth and love of a typical dysfunctional, crazy family. My favorite line is one of Lainie Kazan's, who plays the matriarch of the family. When her daughter tells her that the man is the head of the family, and therefore it is up to him to make decisions, Kazan replies, "This may be true: the man is the head, but the woman is the neck—and she can turn the head any way she wants."

It's true! If there is one thing I have learned after twenty-five years of marriage, as well as from being the father of a daughter (and a son), women should, and do, make a number of the most important decisions in a household.

Women, on average, live longer than men, and they are gaining economic power like never before. These trends are likely to continue. So why am I writing this book, you may ask? Our female clients are typically introduced to our firm by their friends. Why do they become clients? Partly because they know we are good at what we do. But I believe the biggest reason they become clients is that they know I will treat their money as if it were my own mother's. This is no false claim—I actually show my clients my mother's portfolio so they can see the work I do for one of the most important women in my world. It's how I will work for them as well.

I know women, and I know about women and finances. Early in my career, I worked with a client named Deborah. Deborah was a successful, high-powered fashion industry executive who made and spent a lot of money. During our first meeting, I asked her what her greatest financial worry was. She smiled and said, "Oh, that's easy. My biggest fear is becoming the 'Best Dressed Bag Lady in Manhattan.'"

I laughed, but this high-powered, financially impressive woman was serious: Despite her position, her success, her bank account, and her investments, she feared homelessness, hunger, and financial ruin.

At that point in my career, I was too young and immature to realize that the message she delivered to me that day was one I would eventually build the bulk of my practice around. As I dug deeper to find the source of Deborah's seemingly unfounded fear and pain in regards to money, she admitted to never in her life having had a budget or a consistent saving plan. "I have no discipline," she said. We then set our first goal: We would develop a written, detailed budget—which would be the start of her financial plan.

A few weeks later, when Deborah came in for her first budget-setting appointment, she was wearing a new fur coat. Jokingly, I asked her how the "Best Dressed Bag Lady in Manhattan" could afford such a purchase. She replied in all seriousness, "I know we're going to start this budget thing today, so I decided to splurge before getting started." While not thrilled with her shopping binge, I took her showing up for her first appointment as a sincere sign of her commitment to change.

Women like Deborah are more common today than ever, across all income brackets and all professions. Multiple studies have been done on women's biggest fears when it comes to money and on women's relationship to financial planning, and believe it or not, Bag Lady Syndrome (BLS) has been identified as women's number one financial fear. In fact, one *USA Today* study revealed that over 50 percent of women in the United States fear becoming a "bag lady." The number one thing—after losing a spouse—that keeps more than 50 percent of women up at night is the fear of running out of money after retirement.

The majority of women—from stay-at-home moms to CEOs—have a unique relationship to their money and financial planning. One of the most important concepts I have learned in my thirty years of experience is that I need to actively listen to all my prospective clients to understand their true fears and anxieties relating to their money. Typically, I need to dig in like a therapist to get to the root of their concerns.

Too many women have told me about experiences with other financial advisors who have handed them a recommended portfolio or stock market product at the end of the first meeting, without bothering to ask questions or listen. My goal for the initial client meeting is to have my clients leave with the feeling that finally someone is listening to their concerns and, more importantly, understands their particular issues and is qualified to address them.

Over the years, many of my clients, friends, and business colleagues have suggested that—given my success and expertise in helping my female clients—I write a book that lays out our approach toward helping women achieve their financial goals. Up to this point in my life, running a business and being involved with my family and community left me little time to write this epic book. Today, with my kids almost through college, I found that I had the time to spend on drafting my opus, which explains Drucker

Wealth Management's approach to helping our female clients achieve their own financial peace of mind.

I am fairly confident that the experience I have gained over the past quarter of a century—in meeting with literally thousands of women—has given me valuable insight into what keeps them up at night and how to fix their problems. In client meetings I always explain the Three Es that set Drucker Wealth Management apart from the rest.

Experience—I have been in this business for almost thirty years, and probably longer if you consider I grew up with a dad in the business. It takes a decade to master any complex body of knowledge and ten thousand hours to develop skillful work habits and discipline. A lot can be said for firms that embrace the master/apprentice team-based approach, like the one we have had in place at Drucker Wealth Management since I first joined forces with my father.

Education—I am a chartered financial consultant and a chartered life underwriter, I have a certificate in Retirement Income Planning from the Wharton School, and I have a BS in accounting and finance. I often tell my clients none of this makes me the smartest person in the room, but it does show I have gone further down the educational path than the typical financial advisor.

Exceeding Expectation—We all like to do business with successful people. I want my doctor, dentist, and accountant to be the tops in their fields. I have been recognized by Hornor, Townsend & Kent, Inc. (HTK)[1], my securities broker-dealer, as the number one advisory firm in the country for the past seven years. In fact, of HTK's approximately one thousand advisors throughout the United States, I am the first advisor in the company's history to achieve this honor. I have also been selected as a multiple-year winner of the prestigious Five Star Wealth Manager Award[2], meaning that I have satisfied ten specific objectives as set by stringent evaluation criteria. Indeed, only 7 percent of all wealth managers in the United States qualify for this award. Finally, I was recently awarded the Women's Choice Award for Financial Advisors. This is especially meaningful as it validates the work we do for our female clients.[3]

---

1 Lance offers securities and investment advisor services through Hornor, Townsend and Kent, Inc., (HTK), Registered Investment Advisor, Member of FINRA and SIPC, 2 Park Ave, Suite 300, New York, NY 10016. (212) 697-1355. Drucker Wealth Management is independent of HTK. HTK does not offer tax or legal advice.

2 The overall evaluation score of a wealth manager reflects an average of all respondents and may not be representative of any one client's evaluation. The award is not indicative of the wealth manager's future performance. For more information on the FIVE STAR Award and the research/selection methodology, go to: www.fivestarprofessional.com/WMSummaryandResearch.pdf

3 The Women's Choice Award Financial Advisor program was created by WomenCertified Inc., the Voice of Women, in an effort to help women make smart financial choices. The program is based on seventeen objective criteria associated with providing quality service to women clients such as credentials, experience and a favorable regulatory history, among other factors. Financial advisors do not pay a fee to be considered or placed on the final list of Women's Choice Award® Financial Advisors, though they may have paid a basic program fee to cover the cost of a client survey through Advisor Impact. The inclusion of a financial advisor within the Women's Choice Award Financial Advisor network should not be construed as an endorsement of the financial advisor by WomenCertified or its partners and affiliates and is no guarantee as to future investment success.

I don't assume that reading this book or hiring my firm as your wealth manager is going to help you achieve all your life goals. But having a smart, experienced advisor walk you through all possible impacts of the various financial, investment, housing, insurance, retirement, and healthcare options available can help empower you and can lead to better decision making over the long-term.

CHAPTER 2

Who Is the Boogeyman
Under Your Bed?

Money is better than poverty, if only for financial reasons.

—WOODY ALLEN

When potential clients visit my office for the first time, I don't assume their purpose is to choose me as their financial advisor in that initial meeting. After three decades of meeting with all types of clients, I've found that what most potential clients want is someone with the ability to listen closely and actually hear what they are saying—and, more importantly, to understand the feelings behind their words.

Before I can consider helping a client, I take the time to learn a few very important things about her. My goal is to figure out my clients' pain points and get to the root of these points by asking the following questions:

- What types of money issues or problems are keeping you awake at night?
- What has changed in your life recently?
- What prompted you to come here to see me?
- Why are you coming to see me *now*?
- What has been your biggest financial mistake?

All of these questions are just a different version of, "What's really bothering you?"

During this get-acquainted process, I listen carefully, with an open mind, rather than wait for an opportunity to jump in and speak.

Her Real Financial Terrors

Once we begin to hit the root of a client's pain, the truth about what matters most to her begins to spill out. Responses I often hear include the following:

- I'm terrified I will outlive my money and am worried I will become a bag lady.
- I can't understand my financial statements. I have no idea what I own.
- I'm worried about another Great Depression, like the one my parents (or grandparents) lived through.
- I'm concerned about losing my financial independence because of making wrong decisions.

- I've accumulated a number of stocks, mutual funds, etc.—but have no real financial plan.
- I think I'm paying too much in investment fees, but I have no idea what I'm paying.
- Whenever I try to reach my current financial advisor, it takes a week to hear back.
- I'm worried about the financial impact of losing my job.
- I'm coming up on the age at which Social Security begins, but I have no idea when the optimum time is to start my benefits.
- My mother lived into her nineties. If I live that long, I'm scared there will be no one to take care of me.
- I am terrified of losing my independence.
- I have no idea how to turn my savings and investments into retirement income.
- I don't know how to protect against inflation.
- All my friends seem to be profiting from their investments, but everything I touch loses value.

The list is long, and we will get to the details of each issue throughout the course of this book. The takeaway at this point is this: My role as an advisor is to help clients understand that their fears are not unique, and there are a number of ways I can help mitigate, if not take away, those fears.

Revealing Vulnerabilities

I have found that most women are significantly more likely than men to share their fears and vulnerabilities, in particular when it comes to their perceived—or real—lack of knowledge about financial issues. For example, when women say they can't understand their financial statements, I ask why that situation has come to pass. The reality is quite simple: In many cases their financial advisors never took the time to explain how to read a monthly statement. In many cases, these women have not even *opened* their statements for the last few months. During volatile markets, they are simply too terrified of what may lie inside.

When women are concerned about the next Great Depression or losing their financial independence, it's often because they grew up in family environments where financial security was never stable.

When a woman is worried about outliving her money, it may be because she never created a financial or goal plan, and therefore has no idea how long her money will actually last. Anxiety over not having a plan in place may just mean that she has listened to too many opinions regarding investments. Confusion and bad experiences can lead to either ignoring finances or over-thinking them to the point of paralysis.

There are always valid reasons behind the financial pain women feel. Taking the time to dig those reasons up and discuss them is the first step toward laying them to rest.

From Macro Anxieties to *Laverne and Shirley*

In the opening chapter, we discussed BLS (Bag Lady Syndrome), which is real, but does not often end in reality. Most women never become the bag lady they fear they'll become. But other anxieties are much more founded, and thus, actually easier to resolve:

- *Global anxieties*—Some women come into my office paralyzed by what I call "macro fears," such as global warming, the decline of the United States as a global superpower, the spiraling federal deficit, or the failure of federal policies and programs. These stories are hard to ignore in today's media-saturated world—even if only 50 percent of the facts and statistics being quoted are true. My response to these concerns about the *crisis du jour* is that more often than not, the feared crisis actually does not come to pass. Look at what happened with the Y2K scare. Of course there will be events that will shake world markets to their very foundations, but the fact remains that in the past century our nation has survived a Great Depression, two World Wars, the Cold War, the dot-com bust, and the most recent banking and financial systems meltdown of 2008/9. Despite all the tough times, I tell clients, we pull through.

- *Diversification and hedging*—Many investors can be overexposed to whatever their "boogeyman under the bed" may be. For example, if they lie awake at night worrying about rising inflation, it may be because they are sitting on too much cash and fixed income. So while they understand the risks of inflation, because they are scared of market volatility, they are making the mistake of not owning enough equities or other asset classes, which can provide the inflation hedge they need. This is where my providing education, historical perspective, and a bucketing strategy for their money helps assuage fears.

- *The cost of doing business*—Whenever clients tell me they think they are paying financial advisors too much in fees, I try to first address the concern by analyzing exactly what they are paying—taking into account advisor fees, management fees, operating costs, trading costs, and so on. In many cases, they are not paying an egregious amount, but the real problem behind their worry is the more general fear of having put their trust in someone only to find out it was misplaced. Either the advisor has never explained exactly how he is compensated, or he has obfuscated when asked. An advisor's required job is to provide clarity on how he is compensated.

I tell my clients who feel they are being ripped off by financial advisors that there is always a way to invest with no cost at all. Each day, you can turn on CNBC and watch *Mad Money*, where various stocks du jour are promoted, absolutely for free. The problem is that on the whole, the stock picks touted on that show have had a mostly dismal track record. The show is pure entertainment and has nothing to do with serving individual clients or building their trust. You get the trust you pay for—and you deserve the trust you pay for.

- *The power of education*—In response to one of the first questions I ask during my first meeting with a new client—"How do you feel about money?"—I often hear some variation of "anxious, dumb, and confused." Female clients tell me this far more often than male clients (men like to think we know everything about everything). Quite often when these female clients were growing up, money and financial issues were not discussed. Many of my widowed or divorced female clients had always let their spouses take care of the finances.

  By the time these clients get to me, they need more than impartial, unbiased information. Many women feel vulnerable with financial product salespeople, and this vulnerability increases their fears about shopping for advisors and financial planning services. Drucker Wealth Management offers clients a true say in big-picture decisions, and we empower clients with the knowledge that allows them to have greater say in making those decisions. We don't expect to give each and every client an F.U.—that is, what one Wharton Business School professor termed, "Full Understanding"—but we do strive to provide enough guidance and enough options so that the client feels confident and comfortable to move forward.

- *Strategies for schlemiels and schlemazels*—Finally, let's talk about the advice I give to the person who laments, "Every investment I touch goes down in value." I've heard this from both men and women more often than you might think, and it usually represents a combination of chronic mistakes combined with deep pessimism. I explain the difference between *schlemiels* and *schlemazels*. These two Yiddish terms, which you may remember from the opening theme song of the hit TV show *Laverne and Shirley*, describe people who are either clumsy and inept (schlemiel) or who constantly suffer bad luck (schlemazel). The schlemiel is the friend who goes to the party and gets so drunk they get sick; the schlemazel is the friend the schlemiel gets sick on.

For clients who feel like schlemiels or schlemazels, the most important step they can take is to start paying attention to their behavior in regards to money, which typically is the cause of all their unhappiness. In investing terms, the schlemiel is the person who gets into the stock market right before it goes down, and the schlemazel is the one who sells at the very bottom.

A good advisor always has a plan. One simple and smart way to prevent schlemiels and schlemazels from shooting themselves in the foot, is the idea of dollar-cost averaging (DCA). In DCA, instead of jumping into a volatile stock market all at once, an investor will feed money in gradually, through a fixed dollar amount, every month or every quarter. No, we don't know where the market will be in a month or a year, but based on history we can be fairly sure it will be higher in ten years than it is now. With DCA, former schlemiels and schlemazels will be buying more shares of stock (or of stock funds) when prices are lower, and fewer when they are higher. My clients report that the discipline of DCA reduces anxieties and increases self-confidence.

Most of the above points are covered in our first meeting, though, of course, in some client relationships it may take several meetings before we identify the boogeyman. Regardless of how long it takes, the process of my asking questions and listening closely is critical before I move forward and suggest or implement specific ideas. Helping women better understand the important role their experiences and emotions play in defining their financial lives is invaluable. Even if we can't make the boogeyman go away, we usually succeed in getting him to come out from hiding and be clearly identified, so that the terror of the unknown begins to subside and then to eventually go away.

CHAPTER 3

Your Biggest Financial Mistake Is Not What You Think

The trick is to stop thinking of it as "your" money.
—IRS AUDITOR

You read the *Wall Street Journal, Forbes* and *Money* magazine. CNBC is burned into your television screen, and you hear Jim Cramer's booming voice in your sleep: "You are smart, sophisticated, and yet, poor!"

You consistently do your homework and only buy the top-ranked funds, yet you consistently underperform the markets and your friends. Why and how is this happening to you? Don't be startled, but it's your own behavior! To borrow a phrase from Walt Kelly's daily comic strip, *Pogo*, "We have met the enemy and he is us."

Let me tell you about Market Timer Mary. Mary Jones is forty-five, has no kids, and is divorced. Her greatest fear was not having enough money to last through her retirement, so she actively invested and watched the markets. Mary, who today is a client, came into my office two years ago holding a stack of tear-stained investment statements.

Every time the market took a tumble, Mary would stop contributing to her 401(k) retirement savings plan and sell her stocks. She would keep her money in cash until she read that the stock markets were up again, and then she would invest in the companies she read about in that month's *Kiplinger's Personal Finance*.

Mary suffered because she tried to time the markets, and ended up selling near lows and buying near highs. Regretful market timing is only one way in which investors foul up their portfolios. Other mistakes clients have reported making include the following:

Bad investments

"The condo in Boca was going to generate enough from rent to cover my son's college."

But it was a scam.

Poor advice

"My barber said he made 250 percent from a biotech company, and it was about to launch a new cancer treatment."

The medical remedy was a flop, and so went the company's stock.

Tough luck

"I inherited $50,000 from my mother in October 2007 and immediately invested in S&P 500, which is always reliable."

The S&P 500 stock index lost more than half its value the following seventeen months.

Other people blame everything and everyone, from bad karma to their cousin Irv. These excuses generate anger, confusion, and guilt, and it is useful to get the emotions out on the table. But in each case, the *really important* question is, "How do we move forward and avoid making the same mistakes again?"

The answer is to recognize that we are vulnerable to our own personal behaviors, emotions, and biases. Investment researchers have shown that for any given investor, personal behavior accounts for more than 75 percent of the results. So, the biggest way to change the outcome of investing is to change human behavior. And one of the first steps to changing human behavior is to look at how emotions affect our decisions.

Two Powerful Emotions

Fear and greed are the two most powerful emotions that impact investment results. When markets are rising, we fear missing out on opportunities that seem to be making others rich. When markets are falling, we fear losing

One of the most robust findings of behavioral finance is that we tend to fear high-profile, low-probability events while ignoring more immediate risks to our well-being. To illustrate this, we've paired some common fears alongside the far more frightening realities impacting families just like yours.

YOU FEAR...

AIR TRAVEL ACCIDENT
ACTUAL ODDS: 1 in 567,480
PER YEAR

ASTEROID
ACTUAL ODDS: 1 in 250,000
PER YEAR

SNAKE BITE
ACTUAL ODDS: 1 in 50 million
PER YEAR

SPIDER BITE
ACTUAL ODDS: 1 in 51 million
PER YEAR

SHARK ATTACK
ACTUAL ODDS: 1 in 315 million
PER YEAR

LIGHTNING STRIKE
ACTUAL ODDS: 1 in 9,903,437
PER YEAR

DOG ATTACK
ACTUAL ODDS: 1 in 9,593,955
PER YEAR

MOUNTAIN LION ATTACK
ACTUAL ODDS: 1 in 32 million
PER YEAR

SWINE FLU
ACTUAL ODDS: 1 in 383,758
PER YEAR

EARTHQUAKE
ACTUAL ODDS: 1 in 97,807
PER LIFETIME

everything. Women often expand on these extremes and imagine themselves becoming the stereotypical bag lady.

[4]But fear is irrational, as the graphic depicts. Look at the second part of the graphic, at the financial considerations

---

4 "Financial Realities Infographic | Guardian My Retirement Walk." *My Retirement Walk*. N.p., n.d. Web. 23 Sept. 2014.

that might actually be worth worrying about as we move toward retirement. But do we really give these statistics enough thought?

And how do we address the flipside of fear, which is greed? Greed causes people to lose their natural investment inhibitions when times are good and the market is rallying.

Greed prevents us from taking part of our profits off the table and setting them aside for a rainy day. Greed also makes us want to outperform our neighbors, even if they are day trading micro-cap tech stocks on margin.

The combination of fear and greed creates a "herding instinct," which means that we feel better about our own investments when we are moving in the same direction as the crowd. Wall Street knows that the investing masses follow herd behaviors, and it has built a variety of systems that work like corrals to keep investors on prescribed paths.

Another fear-inducing behavior that drives financial markets is called "disaster myopia." It means that the further away markets move from a major downturn, such as the dot-com crash of 2000 or the financial crisis of 2008, the less fearful investors become. When crashes clear from our rearview mirrors, we are more inclined to follow the herd into riskier situations. This behavior actually increases the potential for big, boom-bust cycles.

Inertia, or the tendency to remain where we are and not make changes, is another investment behavior that can stand in the way of achieving positive financial results. Jane and Paul Johnson showed up in my office with $1 million in cash to invest—but they were stuck. They had sold large positions in a dozen different stocks after the market started coasting downward at the end of 2007. They had lost 10 percent of value from the market highs, but had "rescued" the $1 million they had come to me with and were hoping to use as a base for retirement income. "We never got back in," Paul lamented when he and Jane first came to see me at the end of 2012. "We saved ourselves from the loss, but we never got the upside."

The couple knew the stock markets began to slowly recover in 2009, but they could not bring themselves to re-invest in the market. Discussions about what to buy and when to buy had even created stress in their relationship, Jane confided. The couple knew they needed someone to guide them back into the markets. After I worked with them to develop a financial plan that outlined their path to achieving their financial goals, they were able to get back into the market but in a more controlled fashion that let them both feel much more comfortable.

The above investing behaviors are just the tip of the iceberg. Additionally, behavioral finance scientists have found more than one hundred different investing biases that affect our decision-making process. Here are a few I have created over time:

ANCHORING	CHOICE OVERLOAD	DEMONINATION BIAS
• Tendency to rely heavily on prior information when evaluating new opportunities. • Investor who learned to believe bonds are always safe loads up on bonds even when interest rates are low and bonds are vulnerable to price declines.	• The tendency to choose a less than optimal option when presented with complex choices or a vast number of choices. • Common in 401(k) plans that offer dozens of investment options.	• Derives from a tendency to save large bills (hundred dollar bills) and spend small bills (one dollar bills). • Investors may make decisons involving small amounts with less care than large amounts.
GUIDE PATH	HYPERBOLIC DISCOUNTING	INSTANT HISTORY BIAS
• Believing in a formula for adjusting investment risk over time, as an individual moves closer to retirement, without taking personal goals or risk tolerance into account. • Glide-path thinking has worked to convince many young and inexperienced investors that they can reduce risk in the present by agreeing to "glide it lower" over time.	• This bias is also called "temporal myopia." • It means investors overvalue the earnings or assets they have today, at the expense of those they hope to have tomorrow. • An example is borrowing money from a 401(k) to take a big vacation that will soon be only a memory.	• Believing investment statistics or trends that are based on success over a very short term, while ignoring longer-term results. • An example is buying a hot dot.com stock because other similar stocks have been generating huge returns recently, without considering how many such stocks have failed over longer periods.

So, what impact do all of these biases and behaviors have on investor performance?

Looking at the chart on the following page, we can see that the average stock mutual fund returned 8.8 percent per year over the indicated twenty-year period, but the average stock fund investor earned just 3.2 percent per year. Thus, we can conservatively estimate that overall, human-driven mistakes have caused investors to be penalized by *more than 5 percent of returns per year.*[5]

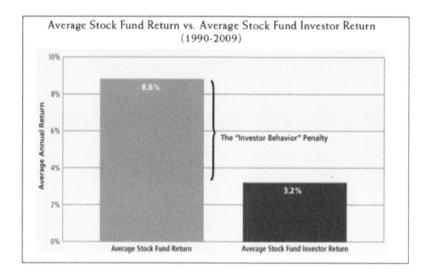

Three Investment Truths to Live By

My most important job as a financial advisor is to keep emotions from creeping into financial planning decisions. If you ask me what the next hot investment trend will be, I will always say, "I don't know." Likewise, if you ask me where financial markets will be several years from now, I won't try to guess.

Today's markets can change unpredictably, even violently at times, and we need a financial plan that anticipates unexpected or disruptive changes. Also, we need realistic expectations about what investments can achieve. With reference to the previous graph, I tell my clients that we

5 Report pulled from Dalbar, Inc., from a purchased QAIB report

are not trying to beat the market's average return—not in the short or the long term—but we are trying to beat the average investor's performance. We do that, again, by first reducing the impact of behaviors and emotional biases.

Here are three simple investment rules of thumb that I offer clients:

1. It is historical fact that financial markets may be volatile over the short term, but historically they produce positive returns over the long term.

2. It is very tough for individual investors to beat the market with any consistency. Many professional money managers don't even do this year after year.

3. We tend to underestimate our future emotions. We think we will be greedy when others are fearful. Fear is a stronger emotion and often plays a much greater role in decision making than logic.

Your risk in investing is not that you will underperform the market, or lose money in the next market downturn. Your risk is that you won't be able to accumulate enough money to send a child to college, or that your money won't last as long as you do in retirement.

Financial planning is not about what everyone else is doing—*It is just about you.*

So, what are you going to do to *change* the way you are saving, investing, and planning for your future? How are you going to avoid making the same behavior-driven mistakes again? How can you personally escape this cycle? Each January 1, Americans make new year resolutions. We resolve to lose weight, quit smoking, and save money. Months later, the country is still filled with fat, poor people smoking like a chimney. So, let's step outside for some guidance.

Look at the Whole Lake

One of today's most authoritative experts on the subject of behavioral barriers is Dr. Daniel Crosby, author of the best-selling book *You're Not That Great.* The underlying message of Dr. Crosby's work is that biased, flawed thinking and unhelpful habits hold us back from realizing our full potential. Dr. Crosby has documented 117 biases that the financial world has created over the decades to herd investors in different directions while at the same time loading them up with information and statistics. The result is investor confusion.

His premise is that the more complex the investment world becomes, the more dazed investors become. Rather than relying on their own knowledge and wisdom, they look for guides and gurus, most of whom are promoting nothing but our natural biases. To illustrate, Dr. Crosby poses this simple quiz:

"There is a patch of lily pads in a lake. Each day the patch doubles in size. If it takes 48 days for the patch to cover the lake, how long would it take to cover half the lake?"

Doesn't this problem sound ridiculously complex, like a lot of the financial advice you hear in the media? But it's not complex if you are looking at the whole lake and not just the lily pads. The answer doesn't even require math skills. You just need to stop, think, and trust your instincts. Half the lake will be covered in forty-seven days. In other words, as Dr. Crosby states, "When you stop measuring yourself by what others are doing and thinking, you reduce your risk of herding." The path to personal financial success, he says, is first to match your personal goals with your own timeline. Then, chart a course that matters to you personally and aligns "your gaze with your goals."

Of course, it takes strength to stay on the path. A while back, several clients called to question our investment prowess.

"Why aren't we all in stocks? It's been a great year," one client said, quoting the increase of the Dow Jones Industrial Average. "I want everything in stocks."

I'm confident some financial advisors would agree to move their clients further into stocks to quiet such clients, for the advisors know that people like to do business with those who validate their own thoughts. People in services businesses do it all the time—they validate their clients' opinions, and that validation makes the clients feel good, at least initially.

But I prefer to keep my clients on their path and remind them how we are invested to reach their long-range goals, not to top some ephemeral market returns.

> *"It may be a time of crisis, but it doesn't have to be a time of catastrophe. It's in times of crisis that human beings are often most creative and ingenious and that they pull together most effectively to solve their problems."*
> —THE GREAT TRANSFORMATION, THOMAS HOMER-DIXON, 2009

Three Pillars

I have developed personal plans for my clients that take into account the following three concepts to come out of Dr. Crosby's research. The three pillars of smart investment behavior are to keep it:

1. *Simple.*
   The investment industry takes advantage of complexity and confusion by advocating biases and herding behaviors. Therefore, the simpler we can keep the planning, the better our chances of eliminating biases and changing behaviors.

2. *Safe.*

   This simply means that we want to minimize losses at all times, and this desire does not change with the economic environment or the way it is "framed" by the media or investment pundits. We don't assume our own decisions can reduce risk or the potential for loss—in other words, we keep in mind the lottery ticket lesson.

3. *Sure.*

   Once we have developed a plan for moving forward toward personal goals, we stick to the plan. We recognize that inflation can impact long-term personal goals, so we base each goal on future purchasing power rather than nominal figures. We emphasize diversification by dividing assets into different "buckets," each of which has a different purpose in the overall plan. (We'll discuss more about buckets in chapter 8.)

CHAPTER 4

Man Plans and God Laughs

Budget: a mathematical confirmation of your suspicions.

—A.A. LATIMER

We all imagine how our lives might look in ten or twenty years; we envision our retirement. But in reality, as we all know, life often offers up twists and turns that change things—for better and for worse.

Historically, women tended to leave the details of family finance to their husbands. When our grandfathers worked, they knew they could rely on the company they had worked at loyally for forty or fifty years to pay out income in the form of a pension during their retirement years. Today, retirement is vastly more complicated, and so is the process of everyday saving and investing. Today, most couples recognize the importance of both spouses understanding their finances. And as noted in chapter 1, many women—through divorce or death of a partner—end up being solely in charge of financial planning at one point or another. Take, for instance, my client Nancy.

Two decades ago, I met Nancy's husband, Jim. Jim and I bonded quickly over our mutual love of Montauk, Long Island, sharing favorite restaurants and golf tips. He was a big, strong, recently retired New York City police officer who still worked doing corporate security. Jim spoke often of his son, who was just starting college around the time we met, and of his wife Nancy, who was a high school principal. Over the years, I managed the couple's finances, including handling the details of several properties Jim had bought and sold. But it was in the last week of Jim's life, ten years ago now, that I provided him with the service that was most valuable to him—peace of mind.

Jim died less than a year after being diagnosed with pancreatic cancer. The last time I saw him, I remember he still had an incredibly strong grip. Shaking my hand, Jim implored me to make sure that Nancy would, once she no longer had her partner by her side, still have someone to help her make financial decisions. I still help Nancy plan and invest the wealth she and Jim built together, helping to ensure she will some day pass that wealth down to their

son. The process I took Nancy through is the same I have taken hundreds of women through in the past thirty years.

Helping women with the process of financial planning after the death of their husband, a divorce, the loss of a job or the consideration of a new one, the start of a marriage, or the creation of a new business, as well as the decision about whether to retire, is what I do best. The time it takes to get through each step of the process—which consists of seven steps that I have developed over my thirty years in the business—will depend on each individual and her circumstances, and should not be rushed.

The Seven Steps

This seven-step transition process is essentially the same for all transitions, though I always take into account additional considerations and certain special circumstances.

Let's take a look at each step in detail.

Cash flow analysis:

The first goal I work with my clients to achieve is an analysis of the dollars coming in and going out each month. In this step, we see how much money is due from salary, Social Security, retirement accounts, pension plans, or other income-producing investments. And then we look at expenditures.

Budget:

This cash-flow analysis leads to the development of a budget. The budget conversation is focused on accomplishing two goals: First, we set aside an adequate cash cushion that covers one to two years of fixed expenses. This cash cushion alleviates short-term stress because it is always immediately available. Second, we figure out how much income we need to generate to cover ongoing bills. In discussing this second goal, we collect all statements pertaining to investments, retirement, savings, and cash value insurance policies. This portion of the budget should include coverage of one-time large expenses like car purchases, weddings, and trips. Essentially, I help clients prioritize by having them create three budgets: one based on covering life's necessities, the "necessary budget"; another based on continuing their current quality of life, or their "target budget";

and still another we call the "aspirational budget," which would allow the client to do pretty much everything she wants to do.

Balance sheet:

Next we create a balance sheet, taking into account such things as bank and savings account, stocks, bonds, mutual funds, investment real estate, cash value life insurance, annuities, retirement accounts, individual retirement accounts, and 401(k) plans. Additionally, we look at the present value and likely future value of certain assets like Social Security and pensions.

Insurance coverage:

After the first three pieces are in place, it's time to review the client's insurance and determine whether the health, long-term care, and life and disability policies are appropriate under the circumstances the client is going through at the time. It's a step that requires consideration of any existing medical issues.

Legal documentation:

Next, all legal documents and titling for properties and other assets must be considered. Titles on all properties should be in the widow's name or that of a trust that will operate in the event of her death.

Any assets that had been jointly held, in a marriage, for instance, should be retitled under the surviving spouse's name. Wills and medical directives must be rewritten, and child-guardianship documents may need to be adjusted at the end of a marriage. If a client inherits a valuable asset, there will be issues of who could ultimately receive this asset, and wills should be updated to properly take these issues into account.

Goal setting:

We now begin to discuss client goals. This is the fundamental discussion that helps me create a tailor-made financial plan for each and every client. Here we discuss big picture planning, such as, "What do I want to do with the rest of my life? Can I afford to retire? Change careers? Go back to school? Keep the family home?" We also talk about any philanthropic plans, or plans to leave money to family and friends—a process which may include setting up a regular giving plan or living legacy. It may also involve more complex estate planning tools.

Financial plan:

Finally, the financial plan is created according to the client's vision and goals. We reallocate various savings and investments to help her accomplish the objectives of the financial plan.

Of course, walking a client through the Seven Steps always means addressing specific transitions, changes, and needs, such as marriage or divorce, sickness and death, career changes or job loss, and so on. Let's run through some of these issues now.

Saying "I Do"

When my clients are getting married, whether for the first or second time, I talk to them about their goals to see if they are on the same page financially. I'll ask questions to discover whether the husband-to-be has plans to buy a Porsche 911 on his next birthday, or whether the bride-to-be might want a larger home. Will they share a bank account and maintain separate accounts at the same time, or not? Will they split bills fifty-fifty? How will they file their taxes? What degree of financial independence does each partner want? Once the couple is roughly on the same page, we figure out a budget for them to live by. It is at this stage that I always offer my best tip, which is one I have borrowed from Thomas Stanley and William Danko's excellent book, *The Millionaire Next Door*: "Live below your means."

We then talk about longer-term goals, such as when the couple hopes to purchase a new home and whether they plan to start a family. Sometimes younger couples haven't yet worked these things out, but I explain that it's critical to discuss early on bigger goals that require many years of funding.

Some couples plan to spend their lives together traveling as much as possible. If this is their goal, we discuss how much they should be saving each month to fund their lifestyle. The old dictum of saving 10 percent of your income has been upgraded to our current recommendation of saving at least 15 to 25 percent of your gross income. The big reason for the increase is that most people today do not have the regular pension that their parents may have benefited from.

We discuss also the importance of both partners making good decisions, and I point out that giving up certain things, such as the daily double cappuccino, does add up. This level of larger-scale and smaller-scale planning helps clients walk away feeling full of positive energy and determination.

In Sickness and In Health

As the story of my father-in-law Seymour shows, death isn't the only tragedy that can strike a family. Accidents and prolonged sicknesses can throw a woman abruptly into the position as head of household finances. When such an event occurs, a spouse has to be particularly careful to think not only about loss of income and how to replace it, but also about new healthcare realities and costs, and how and where the couple can best live out their days.

These changes will depend on the severity of the spouse's injury and the type of care needed. Can their needs be provided for at home with some help, or is adult nursing care needed? Is this something that long-term care insurance, if it has been purchased, will cover?

What About . . .

1. *Income:* Is there disability insurance to make up for a lost salary? Long-term care? Federal aid?
2. *Healthcare:* What will be needed in terms of ongoing medical care? Will it be covered by private policies? Medicare or Medicaid?
3. *Future:* Do we need to move somewhere where it will be easier? Can we stay together until death?

The issues that a woman would need to address if her husband becomes incapacitated are similar to the issues a single woman needs to plan for in the event she were to fall injured or ill.

Career Counsel

Job changes are another transition that require moving through the Seven Steps. If there has been a job loss, I help clients come up with a plan, and in the case of a new job or new job title, we make sure smart employment decisions are being made from the onset.

Any job loss creates giant challenges and requires financial reflection. The first financial task is to consider ways of replacing the lost income. Is it a good time to sell certain investments to boost cash assets that may be needed? If the individual is older, is Social Security an option, and if so, is it the best option, or would it be better to live off savings for now?

The answers to these and other questions can lead to surprising solutions. Change necessitates new questions and creates new opportunities. In fact, for one of my clients, questions like these led to her early retirement.

Judy had been a client for almost fifteen years. During a regular review meeting she told me she had come to hate her job and was literally marking down the days until retirement—which she thought was at least five years away. She also expressed her desire to travel. Judy had never married and earned an annual salary of about $55,000. She had been an excellent investor, not by having invested early on a high-flying stock, but by putting a significant chunk of each paycheck in a balanced portfolio of index funds that averaged over time about a 7 percent return. Our analysis of her combined income potential from Social Security, her pension, and the income stream possible from her investments startled both of us.

Judy could generate almost 110 percent as much income from those two sources as she did working a forty-hour week—and that was before she tapped her current assets such as savings. When I showed her on paper how she could leave her job whenever she was ready, she almost couldn't believe it.

Obviously this situation is unique, but that's the point: Each and every one of us has unique circumstances, and you owe it to yourself and your family to thoroughly review your options with a financial advisor.

During my many years as an advisor, I have also been able to guide clients when they leave one job and start another. In this kind of life transition, it is critical to review the new employer's benefits carefully.

I make sure, for example, that my clients contribute as soon as possible to the company 401(k) retirement plan and at a level at least equal to any company match. I also help them choose which investment and stock options have the appropriate level of risk. I translate for clients much of the confusing health and disability insurance jargon, and often recommend they set up flexible spending accounts that use pre-tax dollars to pay out-of-pocket medical costs. Similar accounts can be set up for those who have dependents that require care, such as children or aging parents. Roth 401(k) plans should be discussed with an advisor, because as some of my clients discover, it may be more beneficial to fund a Roth retirement account with post-tax dollars.

Job losses and transitions are just two life changes I help work my clients through. Retirement itself, of course, is another giant life transition and is one of the biggest financial decisions that we all hope to be able to make in our lives. Deeper discussion of retirement income producing strategies can be found in chapter 9, but we need to talk a moment about that crucial question, *"Can I retire?"*

The answer to this question doesn't come in a single, quick sit-down session with your advisor. Retirement planning is a process that begins years before retirement, and it requires going through the Seven Steps—sometimes more than once. It entails multiple, regular discussions, and crunch time doesn't come until a few months before your final day of full-time work.

The basic question that we all need to ask ourselves is this: Will I outlive my money, or will my money outlive me?

A second essential question is this: How do I turn my assets into a paycheck that is sustainable and potentially increasing?

We will continue to address these questions throughout this book.

CHAPTER *5*

Why Do Professional Athletes Hire a Coach?

Money can't buy happiness, but it can buy you the kind of misery you prefer.

—Author Unknown

All coaching is, is taking a player where he can't take himself.

—Bill McCartney, University of Colorado football coach

*P*remier athletes seek out professional instructors because in the heat of competition, coaching is what separates great athletes from good ones. A coach takes athletes who might naturally be able to compete on their own and helps them achieve success faster. I learned this when I studied Krav Maga, the hand-to-hand fighting system of the Israeli military. I sought out the premier instructor and trained five days a week. It was this intense training under expert instructors which allowed me to survive fighting guys half my age and twice my size. The influence of coaching/guidance can be very powerful, and can mitigate both physical pain in my case, and in the case of a financial coach . . . financial pain.

When I see any kind of professional excelling in what he or she does, I pay attention, for there is always more to learn. For example, when my daughter, Gabby, started training with a conditioning coach at a facility called Varsity House for elite high school and college athletes, I asked the head trainer and owner if he would take me on too. "I don't train old guys," he told me. But I persisted. Six years later, after training with him three times per week, my conditioning and confidence rose to the point that I felt confident entering and finishing a Tough Mudder endurance event—a hardcore obstacle course that has been described as "probably the toughest event on the planet."

Coaches also enable athletes to reach their fullest potential, not just on the athletic fields, but in life as well. My daughter Gabby is a good example. Long before she started training at Varsity House, she showed interest in and potential as a skilled tennis player. At first, she and I hit balls together, and then she started playing in junior tournaments and participating in clinics. After we hired a private coach, we were told she had the potential to play at the college level, but only if she worked to build her strength and conditioning, in addition to improving her tennis strokes.

Gabby improved enough to be recruited as a Division I college tennis player at Lehigh University. Attending such a school would not have been possible for her based on academics alone. Coaching is what allowed her to reach her fullest potential, on the court and off.

Coaches often guide us to achieve things we cannot see for ourselves. I have often used business coaches to guide my professional development and help me grow my advisory practice. Surrounding myself with smart people, whose experience and knowledge differ from mine, helps me improve in all facets of my life—both personal and professional.

Financial advisors fill a similar role with their clients. If you have the time, knowledge, and interest, there is no reason you need to work with a financial advisor, but most people need an advisor. A good advisor, like a good coach, will help you accomplish your financial goals more quickly, with less anxiety, and with fewer mistakes.

I had been presenting a Wealth Management Program to the employees of a Fortune 500 company for the past five years. At one of these workshops, a woman named Roberta approached me after I spoke and introduced herself. She said that after three years of attending my workshops, she was finally ready to meet me. "What changed?" I asked her. She had been managing her finances on her own for years but finally decided she wanted to reduce the time and stress she was spending doing it herself. She wanted to work with someone she liked, trusted and who had the experience to help her reach her goals.

DIYers Beware

As I mentioned earlier, I believe everyone should have the benefit of a financial advisor—a personal financial coach. But what about the "do-it-yourselfers" (DIYers), like Roberta, who have confidence in their own skills and don't recognize the value to be gleaned from others' experience and expertise?

For many DIYers, self-sufficiency is a matter of personal pride and perhaps cost-consciousness, more than it is a matter of actually possessing the necessary skills or knowledge. There will always be individuals who insist on changing their own car oil, cutting their own hair, or grouting their own tubs—but I know enough to accept my limitations in all of these areas. If you ever see me lying under a car, assume I'm dead!

If you are a DIYer, we can probably agree that there are professional disciplines that no one should try on their own. Brain surgery is an obvious example, and I argue that financial planning is another. In fact, financial planning isn't rocket science. There's nothing stopping someone from navigating the dark waters of personal financial planning themselves, and again, as I mentioned earlier, for people who have the time, knowledge, and desire—things could work out. But things could also end in disaster.

To become, at the most basic level, as skilled and proficient as your financial advisor, you would need to acquire, at the very least, basic accounting skills and an understanding of balance sheets and cash flow analytics. Experience with budgeting and goal-planning and income statements is also necessary. Understanding the time value of money can't be denied and ties into the need to understand investment planning principles—which would involve knowing about equities, bonds, alternative investments, private equity, separately managed accounts, and cash instruments such as money market accounts. Expertise in investment management and asset allocation methods would also be necessary for the DIYer when it comes to putting together investment plans.

Tax planning is another critical subject. You do not mess with the IRS. Knowledge of how to use the federal and state legal code to create investment portfolios and living legacies that are tax efficient is critical if you expect to succeed financially.

In addition, a working knowledge of Social Security strategies is key. Did you know that the timing of when you file for benefits can make a huge difference in what you receive from Uncle Sam?

Social Security: Did You Know?
- Waiting until age 70 to take your Social Security can boost your benefit by 8 percent a year.

- If you were married for ten years or more you may qualify for divorced spousal benefits.
- Dependent children may qualify for benefits if you retire or become disabled.
- You can retire, file for benefits, then be offered your dream job, request a "do-over," and change your Social Security if you do so within a year.

Handling one's finances, especially as asset levels increase and complexity of portfolios rise, also involves tackling insurance and estate planning issues, college planning strategies, and even philanthropic tools. DIYers need to ask themselves whether they are prepared to learn—a lot.

The fundamental question is this: Is the value that a great advisor can provide you in terms of peace of mind worth more than the typical 1 percent he or she might charge?

Before you answer that, take the time to peruse the list of eighty things that a comprehensive financial advisor does for his or her clients:

WHAT A PROFESSIONAL ADVISOR DOES

Financial Planning

1. Cares about you and your money as much as a good family doctor cares about you and your health.

2. Asks questions in order to understand your needs and objectives.

3. Helps you determine where you are at present.

4. Guides you to think about areas of your financial life you may not have considered.

5. Helps organize your financial situation.

6. Formalizes your goals and puts them in writing for you.

7. Helps you prioritize your financial opportunities.

8. Helps you determine realistic goals.

9. Studies possible alternatives that could meet your goals.

10. Prepares a financial plan and/or an investment policy statement for you.

11. Makes specific recommendations to help you meet your goals.

12. Implements those recommendations.

13. Suggests creative alternatives that you may not have considered.

14. Reviews and recommends life insurance policies to protect your family.

15. Assists you in setting up a company retirement plan.

16. Prepares a financial plan for you.

17. Assists in preparing an estate plan for you.

18. Reviews your children's custodial accounts and 529 plans.

19. Helps you determine your IRA Required Minimum Distribution.
20. Persuades you to do the things you know you ought to do, even if you don't feel like doing them.

Investments

21. Prepares an asset allocation for you so you can achieve the best rate of return for a given level of risk tolerance.
22. Does due diligence on money managers and mutual fund managers in order to make appropriate recommendations.
23. Stays up to date on changes in the investment world.
24. Monitors your investments.
25. Reviews your existing annuities.
26. Reviews your investments in your company 401(k) or 403(b) plans.
27. Reviews your existing IRAs.
28. Reviews and revises portfolios as conditions change.
29. Guides you through difficult periods in the stock market by sharing historical perspective.
30. Improves your investment performance.
31. Looks "inside" your mutual funds to compare how many of their holdings duplicate each other.

32. Converts your investments to lifetime income.

33. Helps you evaluate the differences in risk levels between various fixed-income investments such as government bonds and corporate bonds.

34. Charts the maturities of your fixed-income investments.

35. Helps handle exchanges, tenders, and special stock dividends.

36. Holds and warehouses stocks, bonds and other securities.

37. Records and researches your cost basis on securities.

38. Provides you with unbiased stock research.

39. Provides you with personal stock analysis.

40. Provides you with a written sector-based evaluation of your portfolio.

41. Determines the risk level of your existing portfolio.

42. Helps you consolidate and simplify your investments.

43. Can provide you with technical, fundamental, and quantitative stock analysis.

44. Gives you strategies for trading options.

45. Provides you with alternative investment options.

46. Provides you with executive services involving restricted stock and employer stock options.

47. Provides introductions to money managers.
48. Shows you how to access your statements and other information online.
49. Shops for top CD rates from financial institutions throughout the country.
50. Provides access to answers from a major investment firm.

Taxes

51. Suggests alternatives to lower your taxes during retirement.
52. Reviews your tax returns with an eye to possible savings in the future.
53. Stays up to date on tax law changes.
54. Helps you reduce your taxes.
55. Repositions investments to take full advantage of tax law provisions.
56. Works with your tax and legal advisors to help you meet your financial goals.

Person to Person

57. Monitors changes in your life and family situation.
58. Proactively keeps in touch with you.
59. Remains only a telephone call away to answer financial questions for you.
60. Serves as a human glossary for financial terms such as beta, P/E ratio, and Sharpe ratio.

61. Makes sure that your advisor & their firm provide excellent service at all times.
62. Provides referrals to other professionals, such as accountants and attorneys.
63. Refers you to banking establishments for loan and trust alternatives.
64. Provides you with a chart showing the monthly income from all of your investments.
65. Suggests alternatives to increase your income during retirement.
66. Listens and provides feedback in a way that a magazine or newsletter writer does not.
67. Shares the experience of dozens or hundreds of their clients who have faced circumstances similar to yours.
68. Helps educate your children and grandchildren about investments and financial concepts.
69. Holds seminars to discuss significant and/or new financial concepts.
70. Helps with the continuity of your family's financial plan through generations.
71. Facilitates the transfer of investments from individual names or trust, or from an owner through to beneficiaries.
72. Keeps you on track.
73. Identifies your savings shortfalls.

74. Develops and monitors a strategy for debt reduction.
75. Educates you on retirement issues.
76. Educates you on estate planning issues.
77. Educates you on college savings and financial aid options.
78. Is someone you can trust and get advice from in all your financial matters.
79. Is a wise sounding board for ideas you are considering.
80. Is honest with you.

Look for Continuity and Consistency

When you go looking for an advisor, whether you have been a DIYer for decades, have experienced a major life change, or are simply frustrated with your current advisor, make sure you choose a professional with a consistent work history, which includes working with the same clients and firm over a significant period of time. Sure, as I have mentioned, there will always be room for new college graduates—we need that fresh perspective. But shop around carefully.

In both the securities and insurance industries, there has recently been heated competition to recruit successful advisors by encouraging them to "jump ship" from their current firms. In the securities industry, a number of advisors have broken away from their firms to become more independent. Similarly, some experienced insurance agents have left their "career companies" to join independent producer groups.

While these trends are not necessarily bad for the industry, you may want to treat a pattern of frequent job jumping as a red flag. After all, if your advisor jumps ship again, will you be left behind?

Insist on a Fiduciary

The final important quality you should look for in an advisor is a fiduciary relationship. A fiduciary relationship means that your advisor sits on your side of the table, puts your needs ahead of his or her own goals, and avoids conflicts of interest with your needs and objectives. A person who earns a living selling financial products may or may not give you good advice and service. But that person, by definition, owes an allegiance to the firm whose products are being offered. We've all heard stories of Wall Street firms that sold shoddy mortgage-backed securities or hot initial public offerings that tanked. When clients sued these firms, their defense essentially was, "You should have known that I—sitting on the other side of the table—am your adversary."

A fiduciary is never legally allowed to make such a claim. By law, a fiduciary may not take actions adverse to your interest and must clearly disclose any conflicts of interest or, better yet, avoid them. If you establish a relationship with a Registered Investment Adviser (RIA) or an Investment Adviser Representative (IAR)[6], then you will never have to wonder, "Am I working with my adversary?"

6 Lance is an Investment Advisory Representative of Hornor, Townsend and Kent, Inc., (HTK)

CHAPTER 6

Financial Planning Does Not Equal Investment Planning

The economy depends about as much on economists as the weather does on weather forecasters.

—JEAN-PAUL KAUFFMANN

Asking, "Will my money be OK?" is not the same as asking, "Will I be OK?"

Investment planning may answer some of the former question, but without financial planning, you cannot adequately answer the latter. Many people don't realize that one without the other is like peanut butter without the jelly—pretty good alone, but great when put together.

Lily was a client who came to my office with a $950,000 portfolio several years ago after being downsized at her job. Through her 401(k) at work, she had been investing a portion of her salary every month, in addition to developing a portfolio outside of her retirement plan with her advisor's help. Luckily, due to the passage of time, more than having any real strategy, her investments grew. In annual meetings with her advisor, Lily would bring her typically unopened statements, and her advisor would recommend certain stocks and other investment vehicles that Lily admittedly didn't really understand.

Lily came to me wondering if she had enough to retire. Her previous advisor told her that with nearly $1 million in savings she probably could, but what that retirement would look like wasn't exactly clear. Would she be able to travel, go to the theater, continue her charitable giving, and continue to shop at her favorite stores?

Lily felt like she had never been given a plan of action. She felt her money wasn't being watched closely, and she didn't feel like she had had any kind of investment strategy—she had just benefited from luck. Essentially, she didn't feel like her money or her advisor were working as hard for her as she wanted them too, and she didn't want to count on time and luck any longer. Yes, she needed an investment strategy, but her initial concern was maximizing her investments. I therefore followed the credo of one of my mentors: satisfy the need, and then work on the greed.

First, we addressed Lily's main concern and developed an investment plan that incorporated our bucket approach to managing money. We utilized different tax-advantaged investments, as well as some hedged approaches to provide the potential for downside protection in conjunction with more growth-oriented strategies. We also utilized a laddered bond strategy to provide sustainable income to her portfolio. This plan satisfied her need to know that someone was watching out for her and her money. But the big question still loomed. "Do I have enough to retire?" Lily asked. When I told her I had no idea, she was confused. How could I be paying close attention to managing her money without knowing the answer to such a basic question?

"Investment planning isn't financial planning," I said.

I explained that her new investment plan was ensuring her money was being properly watched and matched to her personal tolerance for risk, but that the next step was to talk about her life goals—her needs and desires—in order to develop a sound financial plan and make it all a reality.

The lesson of this chapter isn't complicated. Investment planning is important, but it isn't financial planning. If you do one without the other, you are destined to fail when it comes to retirement. Your money and investments may be growing at 20 percent a year, but that doesn't mean this growth rate—or that money—will last a lifetime. The following chart illustrates what a Goal-Oriented Financial Plan might look like—the central question being this: Can I afford my goals? (See chart on the following page.)

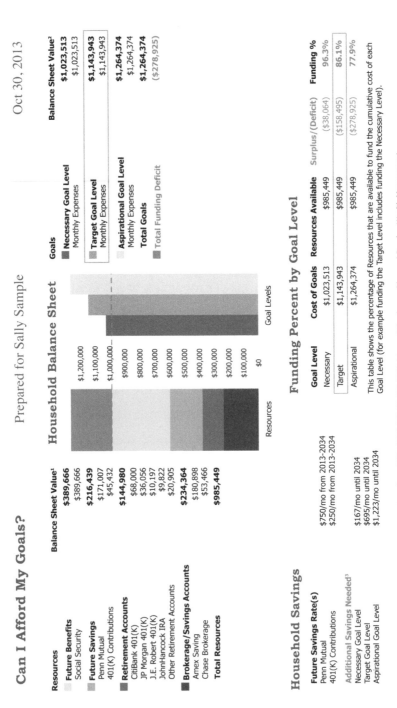

Can I Afford My Goals?

Prepared for Sally Sample

Oct 30, 2013

Resources	Balance Sheet Value[1]
Future Benefits	**$389,666**
Social Security	$389,666
Future Savings	**$216,439**
Penn Mutual	$171,007
401(K) Contributions	$45,432
Retirement Accounts	**$144,980**
CitiBank 401(K)	$68,000
JP Morgan 401(K)	$36,056
J.E. Robert 401(K)	$10,197
JohnHancock IRA	$9,822
Other Retirement Accounts	$20,905
Brokerage/Savings Accounts	**$234,364**
Amex Saving	$180,898
Chase Brokerage	$53,466
Total Resources	**$985,449**

Goals	Balance Sheet Value[2]
Necessary Goal Level	**$1,023,513**
Monthly Expenses	$1,023,513
Target Goal Level	**$1,143,943**
Monthly Expenses	$1,143,943
Aspirational Goal Level	**$1,264,374**
Monthly Expenses	$1,264,374
Total Goals	**$1,264,374**
Total Funding Deficit	($278,925)

Household Balance Sheet

Axis values: $1,200,000 / $1,100,000 / $1,000,000 / $900,000 / $800,000 / $700,000 / $600,000 / $500,000 / $400,000 / $300,000 / $200,000 / $100,000 / $0

Resources — Goal Levels

Household Savings

Future Savings Rate(s)	
Penn Mutual	$750/mo from 2013-2034
401(K) Contributions	$250/mo from 2013-2034
Additional Savings Needed[3]	
Necessary Goal Level	$167/mo until 2034
Target Goal Level	$695/mo until 2034
Aspirational Goal Level	$1,223/mo until 2034

Funding Percent by Goal Level

Goal Level	Cost of Goals	Resources Available	Surplus/(Deficit)	Funding %
Necessary	$1,023,513	$985,449	($38,064)	96.3%
Target	$1,143,943	$985,449	($158,495)	86.1%
Aspirational	$1,264,374	$985,449	($278,925)	77.9%

This table shows the percentage of Resources that are available to fund the cumulative cost of each Goal Level (for example funding the Target Level includes funding the Necessary Level).

prepared by **Lance Drucker, CLU, ChFC** | (212) 681-0460 | Lance@druckerwealth.com | Drucker Wealth Management

Investment Planning: Returns Don't Answer Questions

When a prospective client comes in, they almost always want to hear how well their money is expected to perform. They have a friend who has an advisor, and his portfolio was up last year over 30 percent. Clients will ask about the three, five, and ten-year performance records for existing client portfolios; they will ask to see the Morningstar ratings for my top recommendations. They are looking for a number and want to know how high their pile of money can grow once invested properly.

Now don't get me wrong, these are all reasonable, due-diligence requests. But investment planning isn't just about focusing on a goal for returns. It requires a discussion about the objective and purpose the client has for the money. It involves segmenting the money based on the time frame in which it will be used, as well as the different purposes it will be used for.

To illustrate this point, take my Uncle Bobby. I love my Uncle Bobby, who loves the ponies. Uncle Bobby is always at the track, and he is always up for telling you the stories of how he hit it big. What he neglects to share is how often his horse would almost literally die coming around that last bend—coming in last. No, returns never tell the whole story.

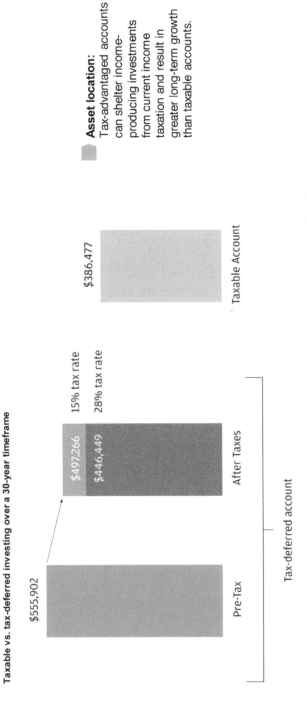

Taxable vs. tax-deferred investing over a 30-year timeframe

$555,902

Pre-Tax

$497,266   15% tax rate

$446,449   28% tax rate

After Taxes

Tax-deferred account

$386,477

Taxable Account

Asset location:
Tax-advantaged accounts
can shelter income-
producing investments
from current income
taxation and result in
greater long-term growth
than taxable accounts.

Source: J.P. Morgan Asset Management. Assumes $5,500 contribution at the beginning of each year and 7% annual investment return. IRA contributions are pre-tax and account balance is taken as lump sum and taxed at 15% and 28% federal tax rate, respectively, at time of withdrawal. Taxable account contributions are after-tax and assume 28% federal tax rate during accumulation. This hypothetical illustration is not indicative of any specific investment and does not reflect the impact of fees or expenses.

Issues Affecting Investing Decisions

Tax Considerations

Of course, many investment-planning decisions take into consideration the taxability of money. Taxability is crucial to consider when thinking about how money will be used in the future, when perhaps someone's income tax rate will be lower than it is while both spouses are working full-time. Taxability comes into play when considering whether to fund individual retirement accounts, Roth IRAs, tax-deferred annuities, and many other savings and investment vehicles. (See chart on left.)[7]

Risk Analysis

Investment planning also requires an analysis of the risk the investor is willing to take to best figure out what investments he or she will be comfortable with now, and a consideration of how that will change over time. What's interesting is that when it comes to a discussion, the predominant factor in how investors feel about risk at any given moment is how the markets are performing at the moment the discussion takes place.

When markets have been performing well and offering a steady return without much volatility, people are more willing to take risk than they usually would be. The opposite applies as well. What is important here is to recognize the natural propensity to "lie" when talking about risk, meaning, most of my clients don't mind risk, as long as their

7 J.P. Morgan Asset Management, *Retirement Insights: Guide to Retirement, 2014 Edition* (2014), 20.

accounts are going up! Instead of just taking current market conditions into consideration, one's risk profile should incorporate goals, age, resources, investment time frame, and personal tolerance to deal with market volatility. Risk profiles are often labeled on a spectrum from conservative to aggressive. (See chart below.)[8]

A discussion of actual investment options follows the

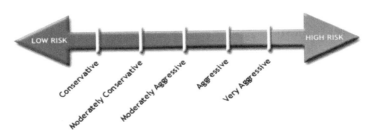

review of risk. This typically will incorporate a discussion about active versus passive investing. With active investing, a manager is constantly reviewing and tweaking the holdings within an investment, and the investor pays for such activity. Passive investing doesn't require constant monitoring, because the manager sets an index or other benchmark and does not make changes unless said index moves.

In setting a client's investment strategy, we will discuss options of various funds in addition to individual stocks and bonds. Diversification—not putting all your eggs in one basket—is key when constructing a portfolio. Different asset allocations follow that spectrum of risk from conservative to aggressive. (See chart on the following page.)[9]

8 "Adelphi Financial Brokers." What Is Modern Risk Theory? N.p., n.d. Web. 23 Sept. 2014.
9 J.P. Morgan Asset Management, *Retirement Insights: Guide to Retirement, 2014 Edition* (2014), 32.

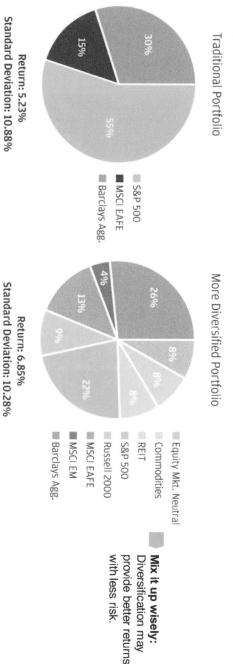

Maximizing the power of diversification, 1999 - 2013

Traditional Portfolio

- S&P 500
- MSCI EAFE
- Barclays Agg.

30%
15%
55%

Return: 5.23%
Standard Deviation: 10.88%

More Diversified Portfolio

- Equity Mkt. Neutral
- Commodities
- REIT
- S&P 500
- Russell 2000
- MSCI EAFE
- MSCI EM
- Barclays Agg.

26%
8%
8%
8%
22%
9%
13%
4%

Return: 6.85%
Standard Deviation: 10.28%

Mix it up wisely: Diversification may provide better returns with less risk.

Indexes and weights of the traditional portfolio are as follows: U.S. stocks: 55% S&P 500, U.S. bonds: 30% Barclays Capital Aggregate. International stocks: 15% MSCI EAFE. Portfolio with 25% in alternatives is as follows: U.S. stocks: 22.2% S&P 500, 8.8% Russell 2000. International Stocks: 4.4% MSCI EM, 13.2% MSCI EAFE. U.S. Bonds: 26.5% Barclays Capital Aggregate. Alternatives: 8.3% CS/Tremont Equity Market Neutral, 8.3% DJ/UBS Commodities, 8.3% NAREIT Equity REIT Index. Return and standard deviation calculated using Morningstar Direct.

Charts are shown for illustrative purposes only. Past returns are no guarantee of future results. Diversification does not guarantee investment returns and does not eliminate risk of loss. Data as of December 31, 2013.

Socially Responsible Investing

An investment plan also can take into consideration an investor's personal outlook on the world. Socially responsible investing (SRI) involves adding another "filter" or decision about whether to invest in a company based on its operations or missions. Some SRI investments avoid businesses involved with tobacco, alcohol, gambling, guns, pornography, or the military.

SRI can make investors who feel strongly about certain environmental or social causes feel like they are putting their money where their mouth is. To be clear, not all clients feel the need to consider the social ramifications of their financial support, and that's fine too. As an advisor, it's my job to find vehicles and programs that will best serve a client's objectives, whether he or she is investing for preservation growth or income.

Holding Periods

Creating an investment plan incorporates decisions not just about how much money to invest but equally important what the intended holding period is. Typically we refer to three time frames of money: short term, a one- to three-year holding period; mid term, a five- to seven-year holding period; and long term, a holding period of ten years or longer. The intended use of the money will actually dictate which investment approach to take. (See chart on the following page.)[10]

---

10 "The Importance of Investing in Equities." The Importance of Investing in Equities. N.p., n.d. Web. 23 Sept. 2014.

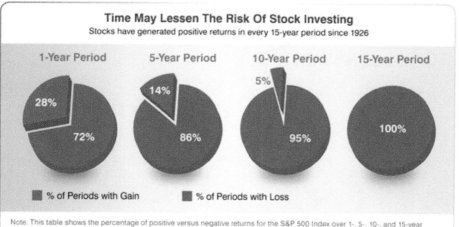

Time May Lessen The Risk Of Stock Investing
Stocks have generated positive returns in every 15-year period since 1926

1-Year Period 5-Year Period 10-Year Period 15-Year Period

28% 72% 14% 86% 5% 95% 100%

■ % of Periods with Gain   ■ % of Periods with Loss

Note: This table shows the percentage of positive versus negative returns for the S&P 500 Index over 1-, 5-, 10-, and 15-year holding periods from 1926 through 2010. The S&P 500 is an unmanaged index of 500 common stocks, which are representative of the U.S. stock market. The data assumes reinvestment of income and does not account for taxes or transaction costs. Indices are unmanaged. An investment cannot be made directly in an index. Past performance is not a guarantee of future results.

Financial Planning: Getting the Answer to "Can I Retire?"

Again, taking care of clients' money is one thing; working to answer their question, "Will I be OK?" is another.

While investment planning requires that goals, time frame, taxability, risk profile, and purpose be considered, financial planning looks deeper at what a client specifically wants or needs—it looks more broadly at lifestyle. Some clients want to know early in their careers how much they need to save now so that they will be able to retire at a predetermined age. Others are happy to work as long as it takes as they are focused on paying for college or for their twin daughters' weddings. Certain clients come in focused on buying a first or second home. Others want to know if they have enough to become financially independent and step off the hamster wheel. So while their initial purpose may be to reposition their current portfolio to relieve their top "pain point," unless, and until, they commit to creating a written financial plan, there is no way to answer their question of "Will I be OK?"

Will we be OK?

Stuck on the Sand

Many people don't create a financial plan because it appears overwhelming. They look out at all the possibilities and potential problems and never take the first step. Not having a financial plan is kind of like embarking on a trip without knowing where you are going.

Another reason people don't make the commitment to create a financial plan is that they don't want to know what the outcome will look like. They may not have been saving or investing, or they may have been overspending and don't want to know how bad things really are! Finally, they don't create a financial plan because they don't want to have to do the work.

Confidence to Take a Peek

Brian and Lauren were long-time investment clients of ours. I constantly harangued them to let me help them create a financial plan. I described the process we would go through to create the plan. They were living in a large home and spending close to what they were bringing home every month. As we talked more about the

questions they would have to answer, Brian began to look less and less enthusiastic. He wasn't ready to start the work it would take to create a financial plan with the outcomes he wanted to see. That said, four years later, Brian is in a different place.

In recent years, Brian and his wife made some changes, including where they reside. They sold their six-bedroom house and moved into an apartment. In addition, Brian inherited some money after his mother's passing. Now that they are in a different financial state, they are eager to create a financial plan because they are more confident about the outcome.

It is possible to just wing it on a trip abroad, or with your future, but those who plan, typically have a much smoother journey.

Considerations in Financial Planning

Among the important factors that play into a financial plan, setting a "target age" for retiring is one of the first and most important decisions. This decision should be based on personal health and even family longevity history. It should also incorporate certain "one off" goals that are expected or sought along the way. These goals might include buying a car, purchasing a vacation home, or paying for bar mitzvahs, anniversary trips, and weddings.

Financial planning takes careful analysis of your current balance sheet. It involves considering all assets, including the present value of future income streams, such as how much and when you will begin to earn Social Security and pension income. It also adds the present value of future savings, taking into account both post- and pre-tax values. For example, the business owner with $1 million in a 401(k) account probably isn't thinking about the fact that that money is worth closer to $750,000 because it is subject to income tax upon withdrawal.

(See charts on the following two pages.)[11] [12]

---

11 J.P. Morgan Asset Management, *Retirement Insights: Guide to Retirement, 2014 Edition* (2014), 9.
12 J.P. Morgan Asset Management, *Retirement Insights: Guide to Retirement, 2014 Edition* (2014), 10.

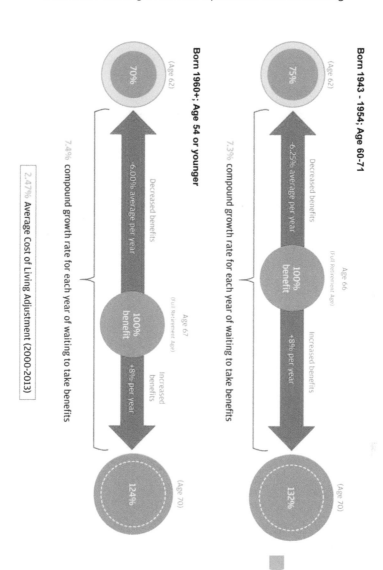

Born 1943 - 1954; Age 60-71

(Age 62)

75%

Decreased benefits
-6.25% average per year

7.3% compound growth rate for each year of waiting to take benefits

Age 66
(Full Retirement Age)

100% benefit

Increased benefits
+8% per year

(Age 70)

132%

Born 1960+; Age 54 or younger

(Age 62)

70%

Decreased benefits
-6.00% average per year

7.4% compound growth rate for each year of waiting to take benefits

Age 67
(Full Retirement Age)

100% benefit

Increased benefits
+8% per year

(Age 70)

124%

2.47% Average Cost of Living Adjustment (2000-2013)

Understand the tradeoffs:
Deciding when to claim benefits will have a permanent impact on the benefit you receive. Claiming before full retirement age can significantly reduce your benefit while delaying increases it.

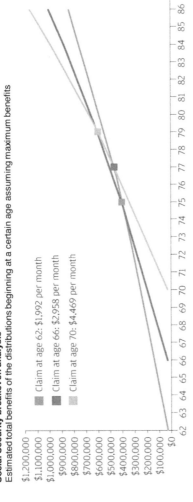

Planning opportunity:
Delaying benefits means having more money to spend later, compensating for increased longevity.

Social Security breakeven analysis
Estimated total benefits of the distributions beginning at a certain age assuming maximum benefits

- Claim at age 62: $1,992 per month
- Claim at age 66: $2,958 per month
- Claim at age 70: $4,469 per month

Social Security break-even data

	Claim at age 62	Claim at age 66	Claim at age 70	At age 65, probability of living to age	
70	$237,120	$187,701	$53,628		
75	$396,206	$403,194	$345,151	78%	85%
77	$466,251	$498,075	$473,507	72%	80%
79	$540,274	$598,343	$609,152	65%	75%
82	$659,262	$759,522	$827,198		
85	$788,529	$934,622	$1,064,077		

Your current budget and your future "retirement budget" can be broken down into Three Tiers based on different levels of retirement luxury. We touched on this three-tiered concept earlier, but the chart below reveals how it works in greater detail. The first level includes "Necessary," or bare minimum amounts needed to fund a very basic retirement. The second level is the "Target Amount," which would come close to replicating your preretirement lifestyle. The third level is "Aspirational," or the amount that would be spent on those once-in-a-lifetime experiences or splurges. All levels incorporate your current ability or propensity to save money both on a pre- and post-tax basis.

Three Tiers (See chart on the following page.)[13]
A simple goal-oriented plan would look at your balance sheet and future income values, and compare those to your discounted future expenses. The plan would ultimately tell you whether you are saving enough money and how much more you need to be putting away in order to hit each of the Three Tiers in regards to future living expenses. Your planning chart needs to be updated every time you meet with your advisor in order to show you if you are on track. The ultimate purpose of creating a financial plan is to create a living, breathing document that helps to continually monitor your progress and provide answers to the ever-present question of "Am I going to be OK?"

---

13 Source: Lance Drucker

Can I Afford My Goals?

Prepared for Sally Sample

Oct 30, 2013

Your Resources[1]

Balance Sheet Value: $985,449

The Balance Sheet Value represents the "current purchasing power" of your present resources and projected future resources listed to the right. This amount is compared below to the cost of each of your goal levels estimated in today's dollars.

Future Benefits

Social Security	$389,666
Total	**$389,666**

Future Savings

Penn Mutual	$171,007
401(K) Contributions	$45,432
Total	**$216,439**

Retirement Accounts

CitiBank 401(K)	$68,000
JP Morgan 401(K)	$36,056
J.E. Robert 401(K)	$10,197
JohnHancock IRA	$9,822
Other Retirement Accounts	$20,905
Total	**$144,980**

Brokerage/Savings Accounts

Amex Saving	$180,898
Chase Brokerage	$53,466
Total	**$234,364**

Funding by Goal Level[2]

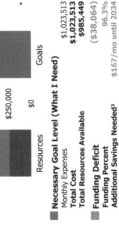

Necessary Goal Level (What I Need)

Monthly Expenses	
Total Cost	**$1,023,513**
Total Resources Available	**$985,449**
Funding Deficit	**($38,064)**
Funding Percent	**96.3%**
Additional Savings Needed[3]	$167/mo until 2034

Target Goal Level (What I Want)

Monthly Expenses	
Total Cost	**$1,143,943**
Total Resources Available	**$985,449**
Funding Deficit	**($158,495)**
Funding Percent	**86.1%**
Additional Savings Needed[3]	$695/mo until 2034

Aspirational Goal Level (What I Wish For)

Monthly Expenses	
Total Cost	**$1,264,374**
Total Resources Available	**$985,449**
Funding Deficit	**($278,925)**
Funding Percent	**77.9%**
Additional Savings Needed[3]	$1,223/mo until 2034

Sometimes the question of "being OK" is relative, or deceiving. Steve and Nancy are both doctors, and in our first meeting ten years ago, we talked about their lifestyle, which included a large home, lavish trips, and a pair of Mercedes Benzes. They were in their fifties and were starting to think about how much longer they'd need to work. That's about when they realized they didn't have very much to show for years of high, steady income.

So, I tactfully broke it to them: "You're going to have to make significant changes to several areas in your financial life." Their initial response was to fire me and hire someone who would validate their life choices. Thankfully, my martial arts training has taught me to take a hit, so I swallowed hard, sat up straighter, tightened my tie, and told them I would fire them if they didn't take my advice.

That was the beginning of a financial planning process that led to the couple scaling down their home and trimming other expenditures, not just on themselves, but on their children. Now in their early sixties, they are still enjoying their life and are thrilled to know that if they choose, in another five years they can stop working and still continue with their lifestyle.

The ultimate takeaway is to understand that beating the market is not the goal—creating enough retirement income is!

CHAPTER 7

The Four Cornerstones to Achieving Financial Success

Money isn't the most important thing in life, but it's reasonably close to oxygen on the 'gotta have it' scale.

—ZIG ZIGLAR

While planning your financial future is not rocket science, it does require a certain level of forethought. An individual or couple must think about, plan for, and then embrace a prescribed lifestyle in order to achieve goals such as a comfortable retirement.

Our firm operates on what we like to call the Four Cs. These are our four cornerstones that we have found over the past thirty years help our clients focus on achieving their personal goals. These cornerstones create a roadmap for clients to head down. Along the way, we know there will be obstacles that can impede progress, but a comprehensive financial advisor makes plans that expect for the best and plan for the worst so that you are armed.

One of my favorite clients, Jill, prior to our actually sitting down, told me on our very first telephone call that the basis of her financial planning was buying a weekly lottery ticket. Apparently, that wasn't working out as well as she had hoped. She felt that she needed a real plan that focused on her goals—rather than counting on the Mega Millionaire Plan. For many people like Jill, even the thought of figuring out how much they spend now or will spend in the future is both dizzying and numbing. And remember Brian in the last chapter, whose enthusiasm for creating a financial plan waned as I explained that he and his wife would have to make a few lifestyle changes. Again, people don't want to look.

Failing to Plan is Planning to Fail

The ostrich approach to finances is dangerous. Many investors fail to look at their finances—or management of their wealth—as an entire pie. Instead, they look at only one piece. Often that slice is investment return, or how much their assets go  up each year. To be clear, performance results are important. But to repeat a common theme of this book, achieving a 20 percent return is not a goal; achieving a satisfying retirement, generating sufficient retirement income, and putting your children through college are real goals that are achievable.

"My guy made me 20 percent this year."
"Mine got me 22 percent."
"If we're so smart, why can't we afford to eat in a restaurant instead of on this bench?"[14]

Investment performance is obviously important, but it still remains a component of the bigger issue of planning for your future. Constant concern about investment performance comes from a deeper issue that can complicate one's ability to draw a clear financial picture and set goals. That issue is greed.

14 Photo courtesy of John Rawlinson. CC BY 2.0. This image has been cropped.

Many people focus on how much money they have—or can make—instead of thinking about money in terms of satisfying what they need. That's where Drucker Wealth Management's four cornerstones help create a sound foundation for finances. Essentially these four steps lead to the greater goal of a satisfied and secure life.

First Cornerstone of Wealth Management: Building the Nest Egg

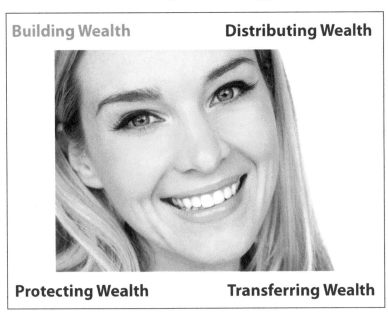

Building Wealth	Distributing Wealth
Protecting Wealth	Transferring Wealth

The woman above could be happy for a myriad of reasons, but since this is my book, she is smiling because she's confident that her financial future is secure. She drank the Drucker Wealth Management Kool-Aid and understands that our Four Cs approach toward achieving and managing wealth is the key to a less stressful life.

Building wealth, as we will continue to repeat, revolves around those two important questions: Will my money be OK? and Will I be OK? Every broker, advisor, insurance agent and other financial expert wants to help you answer the first question by helping invest and manage your money. Again, this is the investment planning aspect of Building Wealth and is very important, but, as we have previously explored, it only works in tandem with financial planning.

Accumulating money over time and investing funds purposefully are the keys to building wealth that will last a lifetime. We use a number of leading, industry-approved software tools that help us create comprehensive financial plans based on our client's budget, assets, asset allocation, and most importantly, goals and dreams for the future. Based on all of these factors, the written plan then can be customized to see what, if any, changes need to be made to realize the client's desired outcome. Our planning software shows when goals are not achievable, which means certain aims may need to be pared back, or other assets identified that can be invested to support those goals.

In affluent communities throughout our country, there are homes filled with people who have been working their entire lives. They own beautiful cars (all leased). They are vacationing at five-star luxury resorts and getting daily spa treatments. They are considered Elite Status shoppers (those who spend obscene amounts of money at their favorite stores). They also are one or two paychecks away from bankruptcy. Whatever small amount of money they have accumulated is invested with experts, and they are no closer to building wealth than I am to achieving my goal of gaining the superpower of invisibility!

Second Cornerstone of Wealth Management: Protecting Wealth

Building Wealth	Distributing Wealth
Protecting Wealth	Transferring Wealth

Protecting Wealth covers two main concepts.

First, there are only three things that can happen to us with regard to our money: (1) We live too long and run out of money; (2) We don't live long enough, in which case we had better have a plan in place to protect our family; and (3) We get sick or hurt along the way and need income replacement and/or enough funds to have someone take care of us. The second main concept of Protecting Wealth is protecting your assets during recessions and market downturns. We will discuss that in more detail a bit later in this chapter.

A fundamental part of an advisor's job is to ensure that they have helped their clients establish the proper protection vehicles that preserve net worth and current quality of life, regardless of other circumstances or events.

Have you made sure that your bills are covered if you get sick, hurt, or disabled? Have your protected your biggest asset—your ability to earn an income? Does your job provide long term disability insurance, or do you need to secure your own coverage? The cost of care at home or at a facility can run over $100,000 per year, depending on where you reside. How long would your assets last if you needed to shell out money over and above your regular expenses to cover the cost of care? Do you have long term care protection? Are you willing or able to self-insure? Because women typically live longer than men, it is even more important that you do some planning to protect your independence both now and into the future.

I recently ran into Adam, a friend whom I used to train with in martial arts. He reminded me about the importance of such plans. Adam, who is now fifty, tore the ligaments in his thumb throwing a punch and was out of work for six months. He's an invasive cardiologist who obviously needs his hands for work. Fortunately, early in his career I convinced him (yes, I had to convince him) to purchase disability insurance to protect those golden fingers—to protect his earning potential.

The second main concept in Protecting Wealth requires strategies that work to preserve and protect your assets during economic recessions. Downturns and bear markets are going to occur over the course of your investing, but they don't have to cause emotional or economic havoc.

Geopolitical events will always disrupt the market and create uncertainty, but remember, our history is filled with such events. The question we pose to our prospective clients is this: "Do you have a bear market strategy in place?" Protecting Wealth involves strategies that focus less on "beating the market," and more on preserving your principal.

Third Cornerstone of Wealth Management: Doling out the Dollars

Okay, so you have accumulated assets, and you have preserved your assets—now it's time to start Distributing Wealth. This woman is still smiling because she is ready to take that next step down the path toward financial happiness; she is ready to start enjoying the fruits of her labors. She now will need to turn her savings into a paycheck during retirement. The focus now is on creating a comprehensive

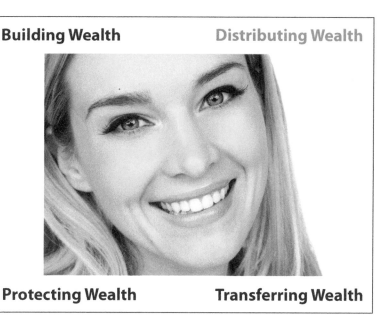

Building Wealth	Distributing Wealth
Protecting Wealth	Transferring Wealth

strategy that utilizes a portfolio of diverse income-oriented vehicles to help provide a stream of sustainable and potentially increasing income through the rest of her life. The goal is to create a stable income flow that provides the potential to increase over time to account for higher living costs, increases in healthcare needs, and other issues, as well as mitigate the cost of taxable events.

Retirement income planning has become a buzzword as boomers go into the distribution phase of their lives. Many advisors profess to understand the best ways of creating income, but few actually keep up to date on this ever-changing and growing area of financial planning. It is important to ask your financial advisor how many retirement income plans he or she has created. At Drucker

Wealth Management, we have prepared well over five hundred plans over the course of the past thirty years. We regularly attend the annual retirement income symposium held at the Wharton School of Business. Helping our clients generate sustainable retirement income that lasts as long as they do is what we do.

Fourth Cornerstone of Wealth Management: Transferring Wealth

Building Wealth   **Distributing Wealth**

Protecting Wealth   Transferring Wealth

After working a lifetime to accumulate wealth, it is important to feel secure that the assets remaining after you are gone will be passed on to your family, friends, and charities exactly the way you want. It would be nice too if you could avoid paying an undue amount to the government. Guaranteeing that all of the above occurs requires a host of appropriate legal documents, including wills, trusts, and health-care proxies. It requires estate planning. We work with our clients within a team environment. We work with the tax and legal advisors of our clients to create an estate plan that maximizes transferable wealth and minimizes taxes.

A situation I can still recall from several years ago is a constant reminder of the necessity of getting estate planning correct. Gloria, who was unhappily married to an advertising executive for a decade, finally divorced him in 2008. She was a busy surgeon and mother of two children. Two years after leaving her husband, she remarried. This could have been a happy story, but in fact, it came to a tragic end—one that was made even worse because of an estate-planning mistake. A car accident took Gloria's life. She had always meant to change the beneficiary of her life insurance and retirement assets, first to her children, then to her second husband, but she never did either. As a result, her first husband, whom she grew to dislike immensely, received the $2 million inheritance. The key lesson here: Make sure those beneficiary designations are always up to date.

A proper estate plan can maximize federal and state tax exemptions. For many clients, especially those who are single and don't have heirs to leave their assets to, estate planning can involve setting up charitable trusts or leaving money to favorite causes. When preparing to pass on wealth, always use a qualified estate-planning attorney. That goes for tax planning as well. Hire a qualified CPA when it comes to tax and business planning. The goal of DWM is to help our clients create a team of professionals whose purpose is to help them achieve their financial goals and dreams.

CHAPTER *8*

How Do You Know When You Can Afford to Step Off the Wheel?

Money, it turned out, was exactly like sex, you thought of nothing else if you didn't have it and thought of other things if you did.

—James Arthur Baldwin

My father's father passed away when my dad was sixteen. This was during World War II, and my dad's older brother was serving in Burma in the army. My dad was forced to financially care for his mother and sister from that point on. Because he had so little at that time, he became driven to achieve his goal of financial independence. He maintained that drive during his whole working life. Ever since I was a kid, I heard my father explain to anyone who would listen that financial independence was defined as a time when you had set aside enough money that you could live off the earnings without touching the principal. Everything he and my mother did was done to achieve this dream.

Defining Your Financial Independence

For most people, the notion, "One day when I can retire," is a random one. They pick a date and hope for the best. They have absolutely no idea whether they can afford to retire, or at what age they can. Nor have they figured out a realistic picture of what their life would be like if they did. Meanwhile, they continue to go to work each day.

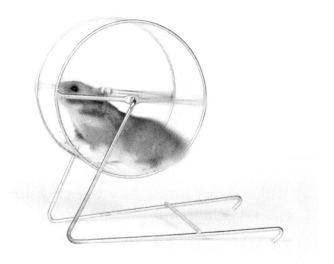

Typically men and women take one of three approaches to how they want their finances to look when they reach the end of their lives:

1. Some want to die with $1.50 in the bank, and they want their final check to American Express—to pay for that last trip around the world—to bounce!

2. Others want to have $1 million (or whatever sum they define as their principal) sitting in their portfolio untouched, so it can be passed on to their heirs. These individuals are often either terrified of outliving their money and/ or desire to pass it on, and as a result tend to live more frugally than they need to.

3. Still others want to leave twice as much to posterity as they have lived on during their own retirement. We have all heard stories about the people who have appeared impoverished throughout their lives but have squirreled away $10 million—which they then give away to charities or universities posthumously.

The truth is that most people fall somewhere between the first and second approach to money.

In *The Millionaire Next Door*, figuring out when you can retire is based on a very simple math formula. Authors Thomas Stanley and William Danko offer this formula to calculate what your net worth should be at any given age, to ensure you'll have enough to survive on when you retire: take your age and multiply it by your annual pre-tax income and then divide that number by ten. The answer is the amount you would need to be on track toward financial independence.

So, a fifty-year-old woman making $80,000 a year should have a net worth of about $400,000 to be on track toward hitting her goal of financial independence.

$$\frac{50 \times \$80,000}{10} = \$400,000$$

Using this simplified formula is a quick and easy way to create a target for individuals to aspire to, but of course financial planning is required to help individuals reach their aspirations.

Unfortunately, many investors (and some advisors) will extrapolate how an investment has performed and then project their future investment value based on that historical performance. Don't do this. The best financial plans use present-value formulas to evaluate the likelihood one will accomplish future financial goals given their current assets. Don't do the Elvis extrapolation with your money:

DON'T EXTRAPOLATE THE FUTURE FROM THE PAST

- ❖ **1960 – There were 260 Elvis impersonators**

- ❖ **1980 – 6,300 Elvises are sighted**

- ❖ **2000 – Assuming continuation of the trend we should have hit 20,000 Elvises, mid year**

- ❖ **By the year 2015, one in four people will be an Elvis impersonator**

There are two important factors in accumulating wealth, according to *The Millionaire Next Door*. The first is to play good offense; meaning, earn a decent income. The second—the one we have more control over—is to play defense. It is extremely important to live within your means.

Most people have to operate on a budget. Now I realize that the idea of living on a budget, for some, is akin to having one's raw nerve meet a drill, as happened to Dustin Hoffman's character during the interrogation scene in the movie *Marathon Man*. Or, being on a budget feels like being on a diet your whole life—which is doable, but not a happy venture.

Many people find it nearly impossible to operate on a formal budget. I am guilty as charged! What I, and a number of people I know, have done, per *The Millionaire Next Door*, is to create "an artificial environment of economic scarcity." We think about and evaluate every purchase and financial decision, mentally judging whether we can afford or whether we need certain things. It's like we are basically healthy eaters who consider whether eating one Twinkie is going to push us past the brink into obesity. It's a ridiculous way of instilling some sense of control in our financial lives, but it helps keep us from sliding down that slippery slope. With this approach, one behaves as if he or she were one paycheck away from bankruptcy, thus encouraging less spending and more saving.

Whether you choose to live your life within a budget or create an artificial environment of economic scarcity, both approaches promote savings over spending and provide the potential to help you achieve your financial goals. The authors of *The Millionaire Next Door* —a book I obviously have devoured and always recommend to clients—also point out the common denominators of those who have learned positive savings habits and accumulated wealth.

TRAITS OF THE WEALTHY

- **They live well below their means. They could have several top-of-the-line foreign cars, but they don't. They could fly on private jets, but they don't.**

- **They allocate their time, energy, and money efficiently, in ways conducive to building wealth. You don't find this group wasting their time on tasks that they can hire someone else to do for a reasonable price, and at the same time you won't see them spending extra on frivolous services they don't need.**

- **They believe that financial independence is more important than displaying high social status. They avoid the flash, knowing the future will be expensive.**

"When is Enough, Enough?"

Deciding when you can retire begins with evaluating your current balance sheet—including everything from future Social Security payments, life insurance, pensions, and other income-oriented accounts to our actual retirement-specific assets and other investments.

Maximizing tax benefits is another key to keep in mind when investors are accumulating money and putting it aside for different purposes. When looking at taxability, a prime distinction is to know the difference between pre- and post-tax investments.

Post-tax investments will typically create a taxable event when they pay out dividends, capital gains, or interest, as well as create a taxable event when sold if there was a gain. Pre-tax accounts, such as 401(k) and 403(b) plans, Thrift Savings Plan, Tax Sheltered Annuities, and most other retirement plans, allow us to contribute on a pre-tax basis, and in many cases will actually take money directly from an employee's paycheck using pre-tax dollars. The money will grow tax-deferred, but upon distribution, the proceeds will create a taxable event on every dollar that comes out. The intent is that money that grows on a tax-deferred basis will grow at a faster rate than their taxable cousins, and when the money is eventually withdrawn, we will typically be at a lower income tax rate than we were when we were working.

Many investors can take advantage of pre-tax IRA

accounts, post-tax or nondeductible IRA accounts, and after-tax Roth IRA accounts. Traditional IRAs are funded with pre-tax dollars but are fully taxable at distribution, which is mandated to begin at age seventy-and-a-half. Roth IRAs put in after-tax dollars. The money grows tax-free and is entirely tax-free upon withdrawal, with no mandated withdrawal age.

The sum of your retirement accounts, profit sharing plans, defined benefit plans, or any other pre-tax program must be taken into account on the balance sheet on an after-tax basis when trying to figure out your current balance.

Years ago I worked with a successful physician who told me her pension account was worth a million dollars. I said, "Nope, it's worth less." She whipped out her statement as proof, and then I asked her if her money was pre- or post-tax savings. She said she took full advantage of the tax deductibility of her savings and had not paid a single penny in taxes on the gain. I asked if she thought the government might want their pound of flesh at some point, and this was when I could actually see the light bulb flash above her head. All along, she had believed that she would merely have to pay capital gains on this money. She was near tears when I explained the truth: all distributions are taxed at your current rate of taxation.

My point was not to cause this woman to panic, nor is it that you shouldn't take advantage of your pre-tax savings, but for the purposes of planning, we must use the after-tax values, so as not to count money that we won't get to keep.

Remember, the longer you can defer, deduct, or defray taxes, the faster money will accumulate. Just to be clear, this type of tax avoidance is very different from tax evasion. As was explained to me by my Uncle Herb, the difference between tax avoidance and tax evasion is approximately ten years in prison.

Another Asset? Your Career

When considering a client's overall financial picture, it's best not to forget one of the most important aspects of success, and that is a person's career. At Drucker Wealth Management, we tell our clients to think of their careers as either a stock or a bond—an idea from Moshe Milevsky, an Associate Professor in Finance at the Schulich School of Business at York University.

Milevsky came up with the brilliant concept that if you are a tenured teacher or professor, or hold a civil-service type job, then your career is like a bond. If you have a stable, secure job with a good pension, you are a bond. Typically, this bond-type client will receive some type of monthly pension—just like getting interest on a bond. There may not be much growth potential in their jobs, but these clients typically have more guarantees built into their career, much like a bond has guarantees built in, and as a result we can look for more growth in their investment program.

If you are an entrepreneur or small business owner, on the other hand, you are more like a stock—with more upside potential as well as risk. As a result, we need to focus more on providing guarantees and protections for them. We have found that thinking about careers and lifetime earnings as an asset class has helped clients with both asset accumulation and retirement planning.

Additionally, we want to ensure that our clients are taking advantage of all the savings and investing opportunities their employers are providing. Many people aren't participating in tax-advantaged programs that could improve their savings strategies, such as 401(k) plans, health savings accounts, and stock options that may be discounted or available to employees on a pre-tax basis. Consider what happened to one of our clients, Lucy, in the mid 1990s.

Lucy had been a talented ballet dancer in New York City. While talented, she realized her career had its limitations. As she approached her late twenties, she decided to follow her growing interest in computer programming and started taking classes at a local community college in New York. She then parlayed her education into a job in Silicon Valley, accepting a job that offered her a retirement account. Believing she wouldn't be in that position for long,

Lucy declined the retirement account offer, and in the end, remained working for that company for seven years.

Obviously, it had been a mistake not to take advantage of investing pre-tax earnings—which would have reduced the amount she owed in income tax during all those years. However, luckily for her, over that decade, the dot-com company she worked for completed its initial public offering, and she ended up with $10 million worth of stock. That's the good news. Unfortunately, there's more bad news, and it is worse than Lucy's initial decision to forego accepting a retirement account.

When Lucy received $10 million in stocks, she called me for advice. I recommended that she keep half the shares and sell the other half when she could, so that we could invest that portion conservatively in Tax Free Municipal Bonds. (At the time they were yielding approximately 7 percent tax free, which for Lucy would have meant approximately a 9 percent yield, or the equivalent of $450,000 per year.) Lucy told me she wasn't sure about investing conservatively—she believed the company stock was going to explode, and rather than flying first class, she would like to purchase her own plane!

You can guess the end of this story. The company (which never had any revenue, as many dot-coms of the nineties did not) ended up in the garbage heap of history during the tech meltdown of the early 2000s, and the stock ended up being worthless. Lucy did end up with another great job, which she still holds today. She is still a client and has been adding to her 401(k) with the fervor of a zealot. Lucy is now one the most avid and dedicated fans of the DWM approach to money.

Containing Fears

The two biggest mistakes that clients make when markets head south are to stop having employers deduct from each paycheck for different savings and investment vehicles, and to switch their actual investments from stocks to fixed income or to bonds. In reality, the exact time investors should be loading up on stocks is when prices are down! Moving into fixed income at that point is like deciding not to buy clothes that are on sale and saying you'll wait until they go back up to full price and then buying those same clothes.

Markets always come back up again. There has never been a twenty-year time period where US equity markets have been down each year. The longer a financial plan is in place, the more it can effectively take advantage of the dips in the market. (See chart on the following page.)[15]

---

15 J.P. Morgan Asset Management, *Market Insights: Guide to the Markets, 2Q* (2014), 17.

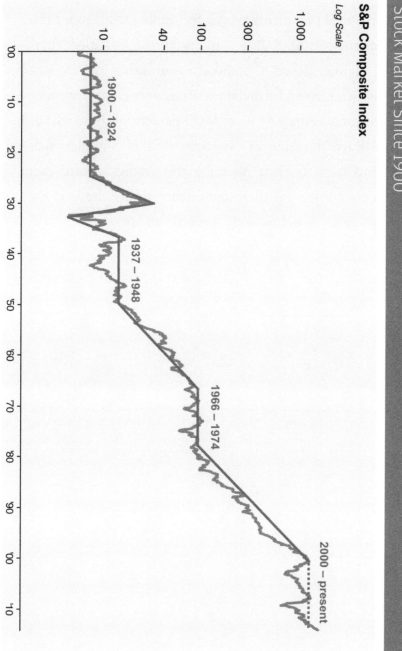

Plan as Security Blanket

A financial plan helps people feel more secure about their financial future. A 2013 survey by the Certified Financial Planner Board of Standards found that 52 percent of those who have a financial plan feel "very confident" about managing money, while only 30 percent of those without a plan feel the same. Having a financial plan in place helps clients monitor their spending and savings. It puts them in control. It gives them confidence to live the lives they want to live—before and after retirement.

CHAPTER 9

Living Your Retirement

October: This is one of the particularly dangerous months to invest in stocks. Other dangerous months are July, January, September, April, November, May, March, June, December, August and February.
—MARK TWAIN

Forty years ago, after she had attended four years of college, the only job Marilyn could find was as a secretary for a large law firm. Fortunately, she had a wonderful boss who saw her potential and pushed her to go to law school. Forty years ago, there were few female attorneys, but Marilyn followed her boss's guidance, graduated from law school with honors, and started as an associate at the very firm where she had begun as a secretary. Eventually, Marilyn came to hate working at a large law firm and ended up hanging up her own shingle. It was at this point that DWM came into the picture.

Marilyn had done a wonderful job of accumulating assets, but had no idea how to figure out how to generate the income she needed as she decided to cut back on work hours and start to enjoy life. This chapter will explain the system we used to help her accomplish this—how we turned oranges into orange juice.

The challenge for many people who have been fortunate enough to accumulate a large number of assets is that they don't know how to turn those dollars into an income stream that will support them throughout their retirement. Their income stream, we explain, needs to have two qualities: First, it must be sustainable so that it will continue to

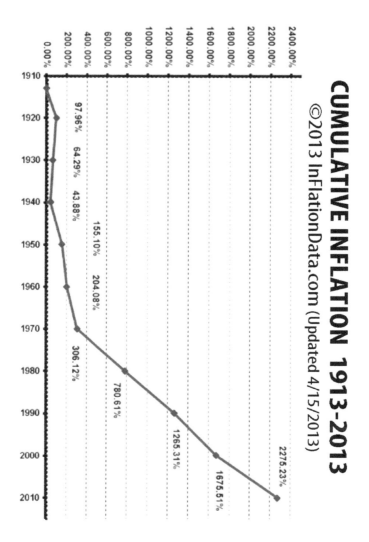

provide a paycheck throughout retirement. Second, it needs to adjust for inflation so that its value doesn't decline over time. (See chart above.)[16]

---

16 Chart created by Drucker Wealth Management, and information was obtained from InflationData.com.

The chart on the following page shows how inflation disproportionately hits those who are over age sixty-five or who are retired.[17]

Will You Outlive Your Money?

This question takes center stage more frequently these days than it did several decades ago—people are living longer. Consider two of my female clients whose situations might appear similar at first glance. They both are single, have never been married, and own their own home.

Rose has a pension from a lifetime spent teaching elementary school. She also inherited money from her parents and has a total net worth of about $600,000. Stephanie is a dentist who, as a result of her capacity to save, built up a net worth of over $1.3 million. On the surface, Stephanie would appear to be much better off than Rose, as each woman heads into her golden years. But actually, when you plot out both of their streams of income, Rose will receive an annual pension of $55,000 a year, in addition to her Social Security payments. Her pension is the equivalent of having an additional $1,375,000 of assets today if you assume a 4 percent income withdrawal.

Rose's pension, when monetized, is actually worth more than Stephanie's pool of assets. Essentially, Rose has $1.975 million, while Stephanie has her $1.3 million. In addition, Stephanie now has to figure out how to turn that life savings

17   J.P. Morgan Asset Management, *Retirement Insights: Guide to Retirement, 2014 Edition* (2014), 12.

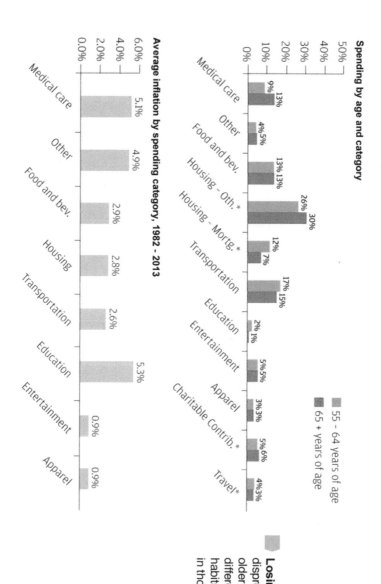

Spending by age and category

- 55 - 64 years of age
- 65 + years of age

Category	55-64	65+
Medical care	9%	13%
Other	4%	5%
Food and bev.	13%	13%
Housing - Oth. *	26%	30%
Housing - Mortg. *	12%	7%
Transportation	17%	15%
Education	2%	1%
Entertainment	5%	5%
Apparel	3%	3%
Charitable Contrib. *	5%	6%
Travel/*	4%	3%

Average inflation by spending category, 1982 - 2013

Category	Inflation
Medical care	5.1%
Other	4.9%
Food and bev.	2.9%
Housing	2.8%
Transportation	2.6%
Education	5.3%
Entertainment	0.9%
Apparel	0.9%

Losing ground: Inflation disproportionately affects older Americans due to differences in spending habits and price increases in those categories.

into a paycheck and allocate to various assets that will enable her to generate the equivalent of Rose's pension each month.

The Three Stages of Life and Money

Our lives can be divided, financially speaking, into three distinct phases based loosely on age, but really more so in terms of what our money goal is for that period.

The first stage is the accumulation stage, which is essentially the time frame that spans from one's twenties to their early fifties. The focus during these years is earning and socking away every dollar possible for the future. While this savings period can run over a thirty-year period, keep in mind we need to save enough to potentially fund a thirty-plus year retirement, if one assumes we retire at sixty-two and live into our nineties.

The second phase is preservation, which runs from about one's mid-fifties to retirement. The primary goal at this stage of the game is keeping hold of what you have so diligently been

working to accumulate for the previous few decades. For many, the investment approach during these years is more conservative than that during previous decades, in that you are no longer trying to grow your assets, but instead are trying to hold on to what you have accumulated and gained in investment performance.

Finally, at the time of retirement, the accumulated and preserved assets must be distributed in a way that provides a viable income stream until the so-called end of the plan, otherwise known as premature death (because really, doesn't all death feel premature?).

Times Are a-Changing: New Strategies

Remember the days of WIN? Whip Inflation Now was President Gerald Ford's attempt to create a grassroots campaign to fight inflation by encouraging Americans to save more and spend less. Whatever your politics are, saving more and spending less is never a bad idea.

Some financial habits and practices do, however, need to change with the times—or rather, the times might force long-held practices to change. Bonds have had a three-decade long bull market, but today it is a different story. Over the past thirty years, interest rates have been coming down to historically low levels. Now, because interest rates move in the opposite direction of bonds, falling interest

A Conservative 2.3% Inflation Rate

$1.00

Today will be worth

$.80
In 10 years

$.63
In 20 years

$.51
In 30 years

Inflation's Impact is Underestimated

But keep in mind, the inflation rate over the past 30 years has averaged 4.3%

rates have meant rising bond prices. Therefore, if you owned bonds or bond funds over the past thirty years, you have received a great total return with minimal volatility. Unfortunately, bonds aren't offering the same potential for gain and yield at this particular point in time, and as a result are no longer quite the hedge that they have been for so long.[18]

---

18 *Inflation: Fourth Quarter 2013,* Survey of Professional Forecasters. November 25, 2013. www.calculator.net/interest-calculator.html and www.calculator.net/inflation-calculate.html

Some people are letting the tail wag the dog, and in their desire for income are chasing yield by investing in riskier types of bonds. So with the thirty-year bond bull market coming to an end and interest rates at the lowest point ever, it is time to review other available income options.

Returning to my client Stephanie, she needs about $4,500 a month to live on during her retirement. Social Security payments will provide about $2,100 each month; thus, she needs $2,400 a month to come from other income sources in order to support her expenses. Assuming $1 million of Stephanie's $1.3 million can be invested to generate 3 percent after tax of income, or approximately $30,000 per year or $2,500 per month (a bit more than she needs), then the additional $300,000 of her savings can be split with approximately $100,000 as a cash cushion and the balance invested in a more growth-oriented approach.

For Stephanie, or anyone, generating lifetime-sustainable and potentially greater income will involve a combination of investment classes and products. The following various asset classes can all be used to generate income:

1. Bonds are debt instruments issued by governments and corporations with the promise to pay a certain percentage over time and promise to return the principal.

2. Certificate of Deposits are bank instruments that guarantee a fixed yield over a fixed period.

3. Dividend Stocks provide regular payments, essentially remunerating stock owners to hold the issue while allowing them the opportunity to capture the upside potential if the stock price rises.

4. Pensions are fixed amounts to be paid regularly during retirement.

5. Real Estate Investment Trusts (REITs) are companies that usually invest in income-producing properties and are sold like stocks.

6. Master Limited Partnerships are publicly traded LPs that provide periodic income distributions from the partnership's cash flow.

7. Single Premium Immediate Annuities are bought with a lump sum of money and guarantee to pay out a stream of income over a period or lifetime. It's the only vehicle that pays more the older you are.

8. Deferred Annuities come in two flavors: Fixed annuities guarantee a certain rate over a fixed period of time. Twenty-five years ago rates were as high as 10 percent or more and now are generally lower than 2 percent per year. All earnings on annuities accumulate on a tax-deferred basis, and withdrawals would be

taxed as ordinary income up to the principal basis. In today's low interest-rate environment, fixed annuities are not as popular as they once were. Although as interest rates rise, they will more likely become more prevalent once again.

9. Variable annuities provide access to stock market returns. They provide the upside potential that the equity markets offer, while also suffering the vagaries of a down market. About ten years ago, insurance companies began providing living benefit riders, which provided the upside potential of the stock market, while providing downside protection of a minimum guarantee to the policy's withdrawal base. These living benefit riders became very popular over the past decade. During the 2008/9 market meltdown, they allowed investors to see an increase in their withdrawal base even though their policy's cash value may have suffered a severe downturn. The ultimate benefit of these living benefit riders on variable annuities is to provide a guaranteed income that the contract owner can't outlive.

10. Social Security Benefits can pay income as early as age sixty-two. Monthly benefits are based on your highest thirty-five years of

earnings. Full retirement age is either sixty-six or sixty-seven, based on what month and year you were born.

11. Supplemental Security Income is a government program that pays benefits to disabled adults and children with limited income or resources.

12. Private Equity is an asset class of equity and debt in companies that are not publicly traded.

13. Absolute Return defines the hedge-fund business, putting to use investment methods that include short selling, options, futures, derivatives, arbitrage, leverage, and alternative investments.

Historically, people have looked at retirement income as a fixed amount that they need to generate each year, but as a result of declining interest rates and increasing inflation, we now need to think of income generation as a moving target—in other words, seeking income that can continue to grow over time.

Another client's situation demonstrates the case in point. Sheila came to me at age sixty-five, about ten years after she had retired. Ten years earlier, she had taken the bulk of her assets and bought a laddered portfolio of tax-free municipal bonds—meaning she had purchased bonds that matured at different points in time. She also used her pre-tax savings (IRA and 401(k) accounts) to build a portfolio of corporate bonds. Fundamentally, her goal was to generate a guaranteed income with no fluctuation in the principal.

However, ten years later, having lived on that income flow during a decreasing interest-rate environment, her actual income was going down as the bonds matured, and even worse, her purchasing power was dwindling as well. Essentially, because there was no growth built into her strategy, she was losing money to inflation. We estimated she had lost about 35 percent of her purchasing power over the past decade.

When Sheila arrived at Drucker Wealth Management, she wasn't ready to bail on her strategy, and we agreed not to abandon the approach entirely. However, we explained that she needed a more diverse portfolio, one that would give her the potential to increase her income and to increase her principal over time. We then structured a portfolio with a more balanced approach and were able to both stabilize her income and give her the potential to continue to increase her principal over time.

The most common spending formulas, both old strategies and newer ones, were laid out by *Forbes Magazine* in March 2014 and are interesting to review.

OLD STRATEGIES

Bombproof Bond Portfolio: Buy a ladder of zero-coupon treasures that mature every year until you die.

Upside: Worry-free guaranteed income.
Downside: You better not live more than thirty years.

4 Percent Rule: Withdraw 4 percent of your initial nest egg the first year of retirement and adjust for inflation in following years.

Upside: Greater potential wealth.
Downside: You could be limiting your lifestyle for the benefit of heirs.

Bucket Strategy: Place enough money in low-risk investments, like investment-grade corporate bonds or defined-maturity bond funds to guarantee a base level of income over thirty years. The rest goes in the stock market or can be laddered to coincide with spending targets.

Upside: Low risk, can be diversified by ladders.
Downside: You could be stuck with base-level income if the market crashes.

NEW STRATEGIES

Dynamic Strategy: T. Rowe Price analysts devised a strategy of 60 percent equities and 40 percent bonds portfolio with an initial withdrawal rate of 5.1 percent, must skip inflation adjustments after down-market years.

Upside: Greater retirement income.
Downside: Income takes a hit if the market crashes or inflation soars.

Deferred Income Annuities: To start enjoying your money at sixty-five, this approach can safeguard against the curse of longevity because annuities kick in for later years.

Upside: Run through the nest egg and count on annuities after eighty-five.
Downside: No inflation protection; annuity firm keeps premium if you die young.

And the OLD—BUT NEW AGAIN
—Strategy of Timing Social Security

The final piece of the income-generation puzzle is Social Security planning. The majority of Americans continue to take Social Security as early as possible. If you take Social

Security at the earliest age of sixty-two, you can lose any-where from 25 percent to 30 percent of your full retirement amount. If you wait until age seventy, you can gain anywhere from 124 percent up to 132 percent of your full retirement amount. (See chart on the following page.)[19]

The decision of when to start taking Social Security typically must factor in your existing assets, your existing income stream, your health, and your family longevity. One of the services we provide for our clients is a thorough analysis using Social Security software that optimizes the best target date to start collecting that income stream.

19 J.P. Morgan Asset Management, *Retirement Insights: Guide to Retirement, 2014 Edition* (2014), *9.*

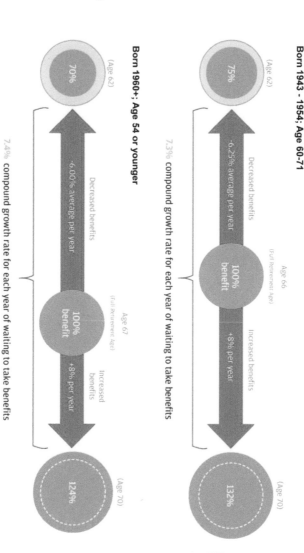

Born 1943 - 1954; Age 60-71

(Age 62) 75%

7.3% compound growth rate for each year of waiting to take benefits

-6.25% average per year — Decreased benefits

Age 66 (Full Retirement Age) — 100% benefit

Increased benefits +8% per year

(Age 70) 132%

Born 1960+; Age 54 or younger

(Age 62) 70%

7.4% compound growth rate for each year of waiting to take benefits

-6.00% average per year — Decreased benefits

Age 67 (Full Retirement Age) — 100% benefit

Increased benefits +8% per year

(Age 70) 124%

2.47% Average Cost of Living Adjustment (2000-2013)

Understand the tradeoffs:

Deciding when to claim benefits will have a permanent impact on the benefit you receive. Claiming before full retirement age can significantly reduce your benefit while delaying increases it.

CHAPTER 10

College Savers Beware: No Such Thing as "Retirement" Loans

I made my money the old-fashioned way. I was very nice to a wealthy relative right before he died.
—Malcolm Forbes

Is College Even Worth It?

"Fat, drunk, and stupid is no way to go through life, son," is one of my favorite quotes from my favorite college movie of all time, *Animal House*. It sure seemed as if college—with all its grand libraries and sororities and fraternities—would be a great way to top off one's high school years. The question, though, is this: Is college worth it, and how do people afford it these days?

The high costs parents face when they are sending their kids off to college have some asking whether higher education is worth it. The entire college experience has changed so much over the last few generations. My dad went to City

College of New York part-time while he was working. Back then, that's how the majority of people got through college, especially those who were the children of immigrants.

I graduated from SUNY Binghamton—a great school then, as it is now, despite the lousy weather. In my time, SUNY was inexpensive, and most students could get a single guaranteed student loan that would cover 80 percent of their attendance costs. In fact, because you didn't owe interest on these loans, you could put the dollars you weren't using for tuition into what was called a zero-coupon bond and actually make money off the deal! But that was back in the 1980s, and college costs and student loans were an entirely different ballgame then.

When I tell my grown children how affordable and accessible college used to be, they can hardly believe it. My son just graduated from Lehigh University and my daughter will become a Lehigh graduate next year. Each of their individual tuition bills for one year is higher than what my father and I paid for, combined, in our four years of college. Who knows what one standard three-credit college course will cost by the time my grandchildren graduate from high school. As the chart below shows, the cost of college has risen 500 percent since 1985.

(See chart on the following page.)[20]

---

20   The College Board, Annual Survey of Colleges; NCES, IPEDS.

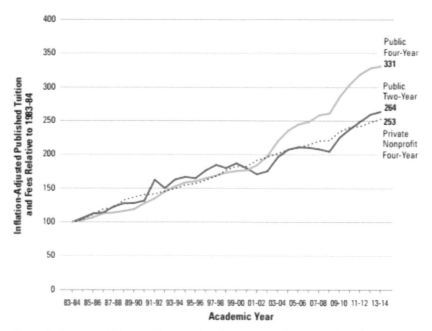

FIGURE 5
Inflation-Adjusted Published Tuition and Fees Relative to 1983-84, 1983-84 to 2013-14 (1983-84 = 100)

Figure 5 shows published tuition and fees by sector, adjusted for inflation, as a percentage of 1983-84 published prices. For example, a value of 331 indicates that the tuition and fee price in the public four-year sector in 2013-14 is 3.31 times as high as it was in 1983-84, after adjusting for increases in the Consumer Price Index.

The cost of college is, of course, likely to rise—it does rise yearly at many schools. Spending priorities are always tricky, though few cause parents as much grief nowadays as deciding whether to sock away hundreds of dollars each month to save for the soaring cost of college tuition, or to save those funds for their own retirement. Ideally, parents do both, keeping in mind that they can borrow to pay for college, but cannot borrow for retirement.

That said, borrowing for college can turn out to be much more expensive than expected, and so it's wise to look at some of the more effective college savings tools and methods. But first, let's take a quick look at how much college costs, on average, at the time of this book's publication.

The average published price for tuition and fees (that is, before room and board) at a four-year private school in 2013/14 was about $31,000, and the average total charges were about $41,000, as reported by The College Board. The 2013/14 tuition and fees at a public four-year college were about $9,000 for in-state residents and $22,000 for out-of-state residents.

I point out the current cost of college in this book not to scare you—though you have every right to be scared—but to emphasize how much the dollar amount has changed, for both public and private colleges, in just a few decades, and how fast we should expect it to continue to change. Furthermore, I offer the briefest of introductions on the value of college today only to help lead readers to the conclusion that where a son or daughter attends college should be weighed very carefully. In the past, much of the discussion about getting into one's college of choice revolved around where the student might be able to get in and how the student could work to present him or her self as the best candidate.

Realistically, these days, the cost of college (and more accurately, the expected return on that cost) should be discussed and factored into a family's financial planning. See

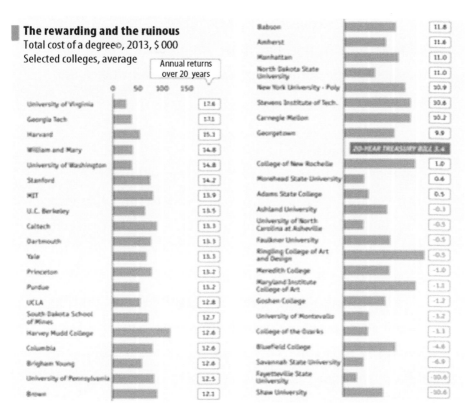

The rewarding and the ruinous
Total cost of a degree©, 2013, $ 000
Selected colleges, average

Annual returns over 20 years

the chart and discussion below for further explanation of this crucial consideration.

This PayScale.com[21] study examined where students went to college and the income they earned after graduating. The results confirm what many researchers have been saying for years: It does pay to go to college, but certain degrees actually post a negative return in investment.

---

21 Source: Payscale.com

So are every college and every college degree worth the money? Perhaps not, but most importantly, when planning for college, some tough realities have to be taken into account.

Saving Methods

Once a family has taken into consideration all of the necessary factors, there are three basic ways to fund a college education today. The most fortunate can cover the costs out of cash flow from income, but obviously, for the majority of parents, this is not an option.

The second college savings method is to begin putting money away as early in a child's life as possible. Opening a Section 529 Plan offers one of the most tax-efficient methods of saving for college. This plan allows parents, grandparents, or any interested party, to invest funds that can be used for a child's future college expenses, without owing any tax on investment gains or deposits. Several other plans, which you buy into with post-tax dollars, also offer certain state tax deductions. (See chart on the following page.)[22]

---

22 Source: Missouri Advisor 529 Plan

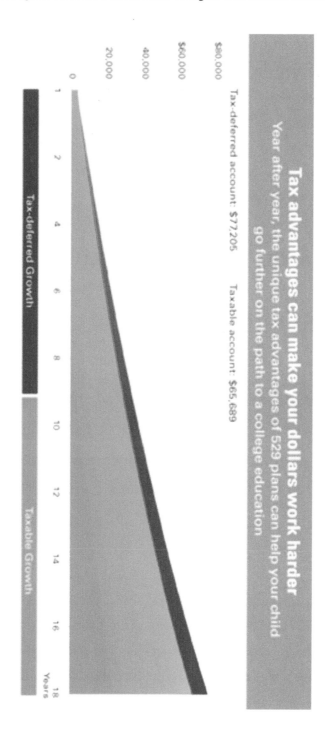

Tax advantages can make your dollars work harder

Year after year, the unique tax advantages of 529 plans can help your child go further on the path to a college education

Tax-deferred account: $77,205   Taxable account: $65,689

Tax-deferred Growth

Taxable Growth

$80,000
$60,000
40,000
20,000
0

1 2 4 6 8 10 12 14 16 18
Years

The third way that families cover the cost of college is to apply for and receive financial aid. Most of the aid that is awarded comes in the form of grants and loans via the federal government, and must be paid back. Colleges themselves also give grants or scholarships, and funding may also be available through state governments and private employers. (See chart below.)[23]

Where the Financial Aid Comes From
Source: The College Board

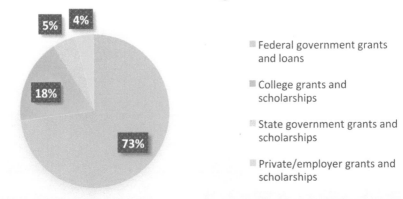

- Federal government grants and loans
- College grants and scholarships
- State government grants and scholarships
- Private/employer grants and scholarships

Federally funded financial aid is awarded by each college based on the answers that families report on the Free Application for Federal Student Aid form, otherwise known as the FAFSA. The most important thing you need to know is that the government will expect parents and students to use a portion of their assets to pay for school. The child's assets

23 *Source:* The College Board

are weighed more heavily than the parents. The government also takes into consideration families with multiple children headed to college. The school offers "aid" in the form of grants and loans to make up the difference for the sticker price and what the parents and student should be able to provide, given the financial situation laid out in the FAFSA.

Some college savings experts recommend using permanent life insurance as a vehicle to pay for college because there is no place on the FAFSA where such assets need to be reported. In contrast, assets accumulated in 529 Plans count as money the government expects that the student and parent will contribute to pay for school. I support having life insurance, though to me, it should be used for college funding only in cases where it is needed, for example, when the parent has passed away and cannot, therefore, provide support.

As I mentioned earlier, aid is not always entirely free help in the form of grants and scholarships. When the financial aid package comes from the college, it includes loans that students and parents must eventually pay back. Student loans, which are provided at low rates and aren't due until six months after the student graduates, make it possible for many people to go to expensive schools. The question again becomes, is it worth it to graduate with a certain degree from a particular college and be faced with a giant monthly student loan bill? Lots of students today are coming out of college crippled by high debt or high debt-to-income ratios.

Americans owe more than $1 trillion in student loans, which is even more than they owe on credit cards. Student debt represents now the second largest balance after mortgage debt, according to the New York Federal Reserve. (See chart below.)[24]

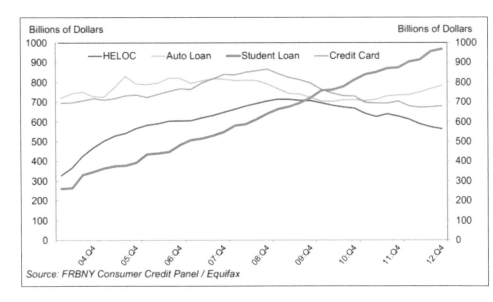

Source: FRBNY Consumer Credit Panel / Equifax

The College Board reports that almost 60 percent of students who graduated with a bachelor's degree from either a private or public college in 2011/12 graduated with debt. In the 2012/13 school year, the average annual loan amount was $8,350, and the average borrower owed $26,500. These figures do not include the costs of graduate school—which was $17,230.

This chapter is aimed at presenting a very rough and low estimate of how much parents, and perhaps their working

24 *Source:* Consumer Credit Panel / Equifax; also found on The College Board

teenage children, need to save in order to fund college expenses. Most people will find they need to borrow some money to cover it all, and I like to remind clients, here again, you can take out loans to fund college, but you can't take out loans to fund your retirement. Some clients think about their college savings as an investment in their own future too, with the notion that their kids will take care of them in the future. But we are seeing a phenomenon in today's "sandwich generation": It is a sad irony that one mother could once take care of ten kids, but these days, often times, ten kids can't take care of one mother.

Part of our holistic approach to the wealth management process is helping our clients figure out the best path to funding their children's education, without sacrificing their own financial future. We are all about smart returns on smart investments and are all for raising the bar in terms of education in our country, but there are new financial realities in sending your children to college, and you should be well-informed about your options.

CHAPTER 11

Preparing for the Zombies or for Whatever Crisis Comes Next

If you're given a choice between money and sex appeal, take the money. As you get older, the money will become your sex appeal.

—KATHERINE HEPBURN

I have always been intrigued by the resiliency of mankind. Ever since I was a kid, I have loved reading books about how the world would end—zombies, the plague, a meteor strike, aliens. In the classic Charlton Heston film *Soylent Green*, future society suffers from over-population, food shortages,

CHARLTON HESTON   LEIGH TAYLOR-YOUNG

SOYLENT GREEN

It's the year 2022... People are still the same. They'll do anything to get what they need. And they need SOYLENT GREEN.

DVD

poverty, dying oceans, and extreme heat. The population is forced to survive by eating processed food rations of "soylent green." Of course, it turns out that soylent green is actually the ultimate horror in processed food: people!

Hollywood is one thing, but the stories that scare me the most nowadays are those that foretell economic apocalypse. Market corrections, bear markets, and volatility are all part of the normal investing process. Knowing that they are normal, though, how do we prepare for them as much as possible?

In November 2008, when the economic system was in full meltdown, I was watching the Public Broadcasting System, and a former Federal Reserve Board Director was asked, "What should people do?" Although he jokingly answered, "Get a gun and a Jeep, and head for the hills," it scared the hell out of many Americans, including Yours Truly.

In his book *Antifragile: Things that Gain from Disorder*, Nassim Nicholas Taleb provides some calming and assuring words to readers and to financial planners like me, who dread news of impending financial doom.

Taleb's premise is that, just as human bones get stronger when subjected to stress and tension, many things benefit from stress, disorder, volatility, and turmoil—including, of course, the human race. Taleb says that when we adapt an "antifragile" stance, we are better posed to not only survive chaos, but flourish afterwards and gain from it. Whereas a fragile person will break under stress, a resilient person will bounce back and survive it. The ideal as a human, then, is to be antifragile, and as professional wealth managers, we want to build portfolios that are antifragile as well.

Look to the Past

Historically, the overall US stock market has been incredibly resilient. Of course, we have experienced peaks and valleys, but overall, the historical direction of US stocks points up, and when other asset classes are added, the results are even better. (See chart on the following page.)[25]

Historically too, when volatility increases so does the actual correlation between stocks. For instance, when the Dow Jones Industrial index spikes, typically because of geopolitical or economic developments, we can see on the chart below what happens with stocks. (See chart on page 145.)[26]

Crisis of the Day

For thirty years, clients have called me about every crisis du jour. In 1987, the stock market lost 22 percent in October, and many clients panicked, but if you take a careful look back, overall in 1987, the market was up 5 percent.

People have short-term memories—it can be easy to forget the frightening impact of the 1973 Arab oil embargo, when the price of oil rose from three dollars a barrel to twelve dollars almost overnight, and Americans were

25 *Source:* VisualizingEconomics.com
26 Sam Ro, "JP Morgan's Ultimate Guide to the Markets and the Economy"
ECONOMY," *Business Insider,* Business Insider, Inc, 03 Oct. 2013. Web. 23 Sept. 2014.

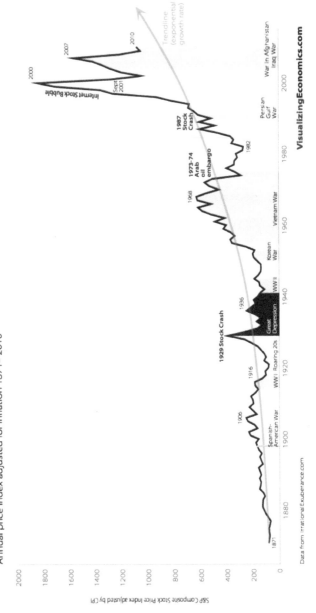

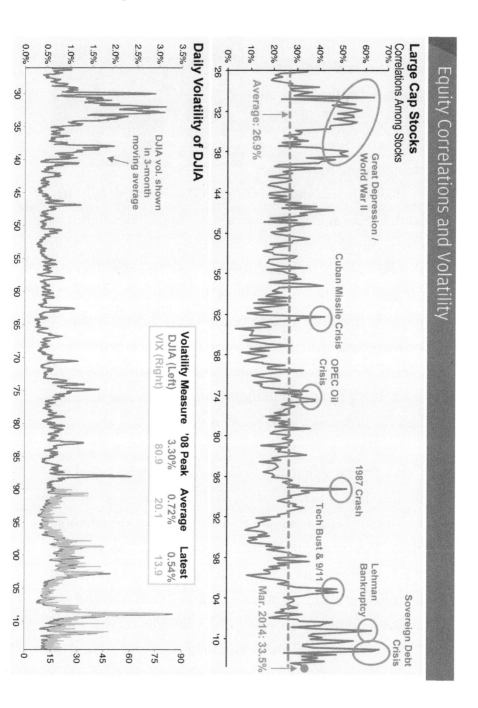

Equity Correlations and Volatility

Large Cap Stocks
Correlations Among Stocks

Average: 26.9%

Great Depression /
World War II

Cuban Missile Crisis

OPEC Oil
Crisis

1987 Crash

Tech Bust & 9/11

Lehman
Bankruptcy

Sovereign Debt
Crisis

Mar. 2014: 33.5%

Daily Volatility of DJIA

DJIA vol. shown
in 3-month
moving average

Volatility Measure	'08 Peak	Average	Latest
DJIA (Left)	3.30%	0.72%	0.54%
VIX (Right)	80.9	20.1	13.9

restricted from filling up their vehicles—when today, our nation is a lead-ing exporter of oil. Time just has a funny way of changing and moving fast.

Recently it seemed that the PIIGS—Portugal, Italy, Ire-land, Greece and Spain—were going to melt down. But of course, they have survived. We all thought in the year 2000 that our computers would fail, leading to massive financial catastrophe, but nothing of any significance occurred. At the time this book goes to print, we are facing a standoff between Russian President Vladimir Putin and the Ukraine. Clearly, world markets will constantly fluctuate and react to the next big thing, but in hindsight, even war and inflation become little more than blips on the screen.

In 2008, a lot of clients were calling me and saying, "This time is different." Consider Sheila, who called me in the midst of that meltdown feeling very concerned. She was frantic because a good friend of hers was complaining about how much money she was losing in the crashing markets. Sheila said, "I figure if Lenore is upset, I should be too," but all I had to do was show Sheila how she was actually doing, and we significantly reduced her stress. Unfortunately, because Lenore had not been a client of mine at that point, she did suffer losses—some of which we have recovered.

Remember, the media thrives on the crisis du jour and panic. The talking heads on the financial channels wouldn't have a job if everything always ran smoothly fiscally. What is important is having a plan for potential catastrophes.

Panic Makes You Behave Stupidly

Behavioral mistakes cause the biggest problem for investors, and panicking is one of the biggest mistakes you can make. When you get the monthly statement, see numbers going down, and then immediately react by saying, "I want out," you are allowing emotion to control you. Emotion, as I have said several times, is not a good financial planner.

For many people, one of the keys to successful long-term performance is mitigating volatility. Investors fill out questionnaires meant to evaluate their risk tolerances, and while the answers, of course, don't drive performance, they do help guide an advisor as to how much risk the investor is willing to take. As an advisor for the past thirty years, I have come to understand that most clients lie about risk. In an up market, nobody worries about risk, and as investors we can pile it on. The first down month a client experiences, and suddenly it is DEFCON one! I'm used to this reaction, and I know how to mitigate it.

Warren Buffett is famous for saying that only in a market decline do "you find out who is swimming naked." Down markets will often reveal companies that aren't built as solidly as we thought they were. Hopefully, you're coming to the conclusion that market corrections are a necessary and intrinsic part of the investing process. Temporary declines occur, but the stock market has historically performed with an overall upward trend.

One strategy to take when bear markets set in is to do nothing. This Benign Neglect Approach will work only if you have spent the time and energy to create the appropriate portfolio before the market melts down.

Bucketing

At DWM, we utilize our Four Bucket Approach to Purposeful Investing. The concept of Purposeful Investing was

DRUCKER | WEALTH MANAGEMENT
NAVIGATING FINANCIAL TRANSITIONS

Four Bucket Approach to Purposeful Investing

SAFETY	INCOME	ABSOLUTE RETURN	RELATIVE RETURN
• Liquid Cash • Defensive Approach • Low Volatility	• To Support Fixed Expenses • Sustainable • Potentially Increasing	• **Tactical** • **Hedging Approach** • **Downside Protection**	• **Strategic** • **Accumulation** • **Growth Potential**

first introduced to us at a symposium we attended at The Wharton School of Business. At DWM, we borrow only the best ideas! Fundamentally it works like this:

- Bucket 1 represents your safe, liquid emergency Money. Your expenses will dictate how much we keep here. CDs, savings accounts, and money markets are typically found here.

- Bucket 2 represents your source for Income. This income needs to be sustainable throughout your lifetime as well as offer the opportunity to grow. The objective is to supplement your Social Security, pension, or other income sources in retirement. Tax free bonds, corporate bonds, annuities, REITs, and MLPs would be found here.

- Bucket 3 is your Absolute Return bucket. The goal here is not to beat the markets in an increasing environment but to mitigate risk and offer downside protection. A hedged approach will vary its investment strategy depending on the perceived market and economic conditions. This bucket would be filled with various alternative investments, absolute

return funds, and ETFs that can short their
various indexes.

• Bucket 4 is your Accumulation bucket. This
is where you have the potential to capture the
upside returns in a bull market. Individual
growth stocks, dividend paying stocks, equity
oriented funds, ETFs, and index funds would
fill this bucket.

The goal of the Four Buckets is to provide a balanced
approach to your savings and investments that, once estab-
lished, doesn't need much tweaking, other than annual
rebalancing based on current market conditions as well as
your current financial needs.

When Doing Nothing Does Great
In early 1973, my father, Bernie Drucker, met a new client named Jack, who had $10,000 to invest. By the end
of 1974, the market had fallen about 40 percent over the
preceding year and a half. Jack, who was a creative director on Broadway, called and asked my dad Bernie what he
should do. My father asked him, "Do you need the money
now?" Jack said he most likely would not need it for the
next twenty to thirty years, so Bernie invested that $10K in
boring, solid funds and told him that, if possible, he should

add more. Jack agreed and began adding one hundred dollars each month until the total invested was $17,000.

When I looked up Jack's investment history after taking over Drucker Wealth Management, I asked him what had happened with his account that my father started for him. Jack happily reported that it had grown to about $310,000. Even though those particular funds weren't top performers, the combination of solid, long-term performance, along with the fact that he trusted my dad, allowed Jack to achieve the long-term growth he had originally hoped to achieve.

Sometimes, a strategy of doing nothing works because the overall direction of the stock market historically tends to move up. (See chart on the following page.)[27]

Basically, over any fifteen-year period of stock market performance, there has never been a period when it's been down.

Three Investment Approaches and How They Panned Out

The following investment analysis, conducted by Russell Investments, compares three investment approaches taken during the financial downturn of 2008/9, and shows how each approach worked out. In the exhibit of a hypothetical sixty-forty portfolio on September 30, 2008 (two weeks

27 *Source:* Yale International Center for Finance database of the New York Stock Exchange and Ibbotson Associates, 2009.

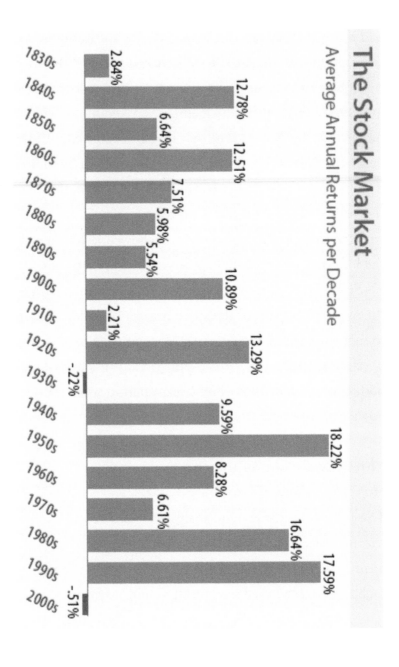

The Stock Market

Average Annual Returns per Decade

Decade	Return
1830s	2.84%
1840s	12.78%
1850s	6.64%
1860s	12.51%
1870s	7.51%
1880s	5.98%
1890s	5.54%
1900s	10.89%
1910s	2.21%
1920s	13.29%
1930s	-.22%
1940s	9.59%
1950s	18.22%
1960s	8.28%
1970s	6.61%
1980s	16.64%
1990s	17.59%
2000s	-.51%

after the collapse of Lehman Brothers, and a defining moment in that wide-reaching crisis), we compare results. The starting point for the $100,000 hypothetical portfolio is October 9, 2007. (See chart on the following page.)[28]

Option #1
Stay invested, making no changes to the sixty-forty index strategy all the way to the present. As of December 31, 2010, this index portfolio is valued at $104,502.

Option #2
React to the downturn and pull out of the sixty-forty portfolio, going to 100 percent cash, represented by the Barclays Capital One to Three Month US Treasury Bill index, on September 30, 2008, and remain in cash until December 31, 2010. This portfolio is valued at $85,469.

Option #3
React to the downturn and pull out of the sixty-forty portfolio, going to 100 percent treasuries, represented by the Barclays Capital Treasury Index, on September 30, 2008, and remain in treasuries until December 31, 2010. This portfolio is valued at $94,451.

---

28 *Source:* Russell Investments, 2010.

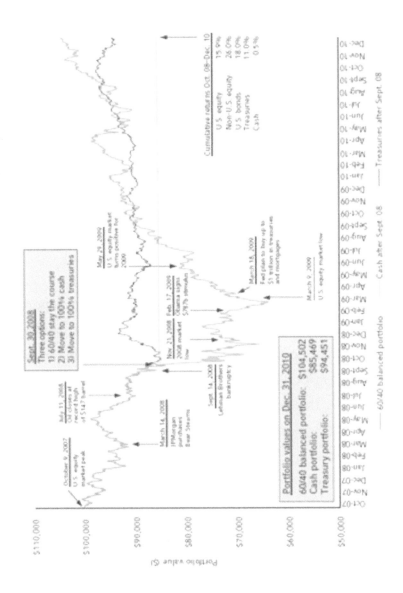

Staying the course was difficult for investors those years, but this chart clearly shows that not panicking was the best path to take. Those who bailed on their investments and moved to cash were hoping to avoid losses in the future, but did they? Likewise, some tried to time the market by selling before it tanked, but did they remember to get back into the market? Could they?

When in doubt, as this chapter has shown, when the talking heads on all the media channels are warning you about the next financial apocalypse and all of your friends are running in a frenzied state for cover, stop, take a breath, and do give your financial advisor a call. And then stop and listen to what he or she has to say in terms of history, in terms of overcoming the crisis du jour, and in terms of playing it smart. Above all, don't panic—fight those zombies with absolute calm.

CHAPTER 12

Final Thoughts, or What's Next?

Money is not the most important thing in the world.
Love is. Fortunately, I love money.
—JACKIE MASON

After thirty years of helping my clients achieve their financial goals, I still wake up in the middle of the night thinking about a client meeting I had that day. What allows me to go back to sleep is knowing that the plans we created for that client will allow her to sleep better at night. I know all too well the unique concerns about money and financial planning that my female clients bring to my office. In my ideal world, no woman of any age has to fear ever becoming the best-dressed bag lady in New York. My life outside my office revolves around my wife and children. My father's goal for my mom, and my goal for my own wife and kids, was, and remains, to help our families become financially independent. My work life and my personal life share this goal.

Changes in our life situations can happen in the blink of an eye—the loss of a job, an early, unanticipated retirement, or an inheritance from a family member. We often deceive ourselves that we have adequately prepared and planned for everything, from that long-awaited retirement, to a declining stock market, to getting sick. It's often at that moment when shock and fear are consuming us that we discover we have never actually developed a financial plan or a comprehensive investment approach to handle these life-altering events. A substantial number of our new clients come to us as a result of these transitional moments in their lives. Others are introduced to us through their friends, accountants, and family members who understand the need to proactively plan before these life-altering events occur. This is often where we can affect the most beneficial change to their financial lives.

My daughter Gabby is a confident, independent young woman. She constantly reminds me, "Dad, strong is the new sexy." I realize she is absolutely correct. Drucker Wealth Management has been helping clients—the majority of whom are women—successfully plan for their futures. These women are typically strong, smart, independent women who come to us to ensure they will remain strong, smart and independent for the rest of their financial lives.

This is what we do.

You have read the book. Maybe you took notes. Are you prepared to take action? Are you ready for that "Second Opinion Review"? Are you looking for someone to help guide you through the planning process, analyze your current situation, and provide appropriate wealth management and investment suggestions? Your first step is to go to our website at www.druckerwealth.com.

We suggest you watch the movie on the home page to get a better sense of who we are and what we do. Go to our client access tab, and click on My$. Watch the video that explains how we provide a dedicated dashboard page—accessible through your computer, iPad, and mobile phone—which allows each client to aggregate all of her financial vehicles on one secure site. If, after watching our videos and reading this book, you think it might be worth a conversation, please email or call me directly at lance@druckerwealth.com, or phone (212) 681-0460. We can also be found on Facebook and LinkedIn.

Thought without action is wasted energy. We look forward to hearing from you.

LANCE DRUCKER is a Registered Representative of, and offers Securities and Investment Advisory services through Hornor, Townsend & Kent, Inc., (HTK), Registered Investment Advisor, Member FINRA/SIPC. 2 Park Ave, Suite 300, New York, NY 10016. (212) 697-1355. Drucker Wealth Management and other listed entities are independent of HTK unless otherwise noted. HTK is a wholly owned subsidiary of Penn Mutual. HTK does not offer tax or legal advice.

The views expressed within this book are the views of the author alone and do not necessarily reflect the views of Penn Mutual or HTK unless otherwise stated. Information provided is for educational purposes only and shouldn't be viewed as a recommendation to buy or sell any particular financial product or service. Depending on your individual situation, discussions presented may not be appropriate.

Investing involves risk, including loss of value. Any strategies represented are not guarantees of future performance or success, and may not be appropriate for your situation.